# Introduction to Theological Libraries

*The Theological Librarian's Handbook — Volume 1*

EDITED BY MATINA ĆURIĆ

ATLA OPEN PRESS
Chicago – 2020

atla
Open
Press

Published by Atla Open Press, An Imprint of the American Theological
Library Association (Atla), 300 South Wacker Drive, Suite 2100,
Chicago, IL 60606-6701 USA
Published in the United States of America in 2020.

ISBN-13 978-1-949800-04-3 (PDF)
ISBN-13 978-1-949800-05-0 (EPUB)
ISBN-13 978-1-949800-06-7 (Paperback)

Cover Design: Simply Aesthetic Design

# Contents

## Theological Libraries Worldwide

# *Preface*

THE THEOLOGICAL LIBRARIAN'S HANDBOOK IS A MULTI-VOLUME GUIDE TO theological librarianship intended for library staff who do not possess formal training in the field of library and information science yet nevertheless work in theological libraries all over the world. This book series is a project of the International Theological Librarianship Education Task Force (ITLE), an international initiative of four theological library associations (Atla, ANZTLA, BETH, and ForAtl) created in 2018. The mission of ITLE is to strengthen and connect theological and religious studies librarians worldwide by identifying resources, creating educational opportunities, and developing skill enhancement materials through collaborative efforts.

The idea to produce a book series on the practice of theological librarianship came as a result of discussions within the Task Force about the state of theological librarianship worldwide and understanding that many theological librarians are working in isolation, without access to any form of professional training or support from colleagues. There are various reasons why this is the case, the most important being: 1) The absence of library science programs or library professionals in their working area, or if a program is available it is delivered in such a manner that a working librarian is unable to attend classes; 2) economic reasons: In many countries, a professional or master degree in library science can be very expensive, and the theological librarians or their libraries can not afford to pay for training; 3) the absence of professional theological library associations in a country or region which would organize theological library education workshops and seminars; 4) some institutions to which these libraries belong think that professional training for work in a theological library is not necessary.

Because of all these reasons members of ITLE have decided to develop various freely accessible, synchronous and asynchronous means of library education which will be offered to the international theological library community. A multi-volume handbook covering the most important library operations and services is one of these means. The first volume gives an introduction to theological libraries and librarians, and the context in which they operate worldwide. The remaining volumes will focus in-depth on the most important library operations such as library administration, collection development and management, library services and preservation, and interlibrary cooperation. In each volume, we hope to provide perspectives and advice from leading experts in the field and best practices from theological libraries all over the world. It is an international effort that we hope will yield stronger cooperation between different theological libraries and library associations, and inspire many new initiatives, projects, and research.

Theological librarianship represents one of the oldest and most complex branches of librarianship. However, in spite of its rich and significant role and history, the topic is in many parts of the world a poorly researched area. In this first volume, we have attempted to offer a general and religiously balanced approach, and this will be our goal also in the future volumes. But because of a lack of published comparative, cross-country and intercultural research, and contacts with local experts in some parts of the world, we could not offer at this time a more global contribution. This is the reason for example why we are missing contributions from the Middle East and some parts of Asia in this volume. I hope the published texts in this volume will inspire more comparative research and connections in these parts of the world, so in the future, we can have a more complete new edition.

I would like to thank all the ITLE Task Force members and authors in this volume for their contribution, advice, and support of the project, as well as theological library associations and their representatives around the world for providing us with necessary information and encouragement to make this book series available.

I hope The Theological Librarian's Handbook will prove to be very useful to many theological and religious studies librarians worldwide, as well as anyone interested in the practice of theological librarianship.

Matina Ćurić

# CHAPTER 1

# What are Theological Libraries?

CARISSE MICKEY BERRYHILL

> *I conceive of my work and that of my staff as a ministry as well as an aid in multiple future ministries. In a nutshell, the text we shared is thematic for me: We are surrounded by a cloud of witnesses—past and present—speaking, dialoguing, sharing with those who would be witnesses today.*
>
> – John B. Trotti (2002)

SINCE ANTIQUITY, LITERATE CULTURES HAVE CREATED LIBRARIES TO preserve human knowledge and make it available to readers. Theological libraries today share with libraries in general the central functions of a modern library, including selection, acquisition, preservation, and description of resources in order to provide access to them. Like other libraries, theological libraries assist and instruct readers, advocate for the relevance of the library and of its resources to the mission of its community, create spaces suitable to the user community, provide platforms for disseminating faculty and student work, manage funds entrusted for all these purposes, and participate in policy making related to the library. What, then, are the distinctive characteristics of theological libraries?

In the first place, theological libraries specialize in texts viewed as sacred and in literature within and about the religious traditions that revere those sacred texts. Some libraries are equipped with the expertise and facilities to collect and preserve manuscripts from antiquity. Beyond collecting manuscripts, translations, and editions of the sacred texts themselves, theological libraries accumulate the literature that grows up around the texts, produced by the communities that respect them. Related works include linguistic and textual criticism, commentaries, theological reflection, and application of the texts. Religious communities generate the literature of religious practice and community life, including ministry, ethics, worship, and religious arts. The memory of the community is embodied in archives and histories of the community, its activities, its controversies, its practitioners, and scholarly analyses of these materials.

In the second place, theological libraries vary in their constituencies. The constituent communities that create and support theological libraries are of different types: local or congregational, single-tradition, multiple-tradition, and extra-traditional. Although no typology fits every library, the main factor that differentiates these four types is the scope of the constituent community, whether in geography or ideology. Often the breadth of the constituency influences the depth of financial resources available to the institution and its library. The library participates in the teaching and learning efforts of its constituent community.

A theological library with a *local* constituency is one related to a neighborhood religious community. Since antiquity, Jewish, Christian, and Muslim congregations have kept collections of sacred books for reading and study directed by the congregation's leaders. Today an example of a local theological library would be a church library with a collection of tools for study of the sacred text, recordings of sermons or services, or videos for children inculcating the religious teachings of the congregation. Its users are likely to be local clergy or members of the congregation who are engaged in devotional reading, worship, teaching, or in religious instruction. Today the staff of a local theological library is usually constituted of volunteers from the membership, some of whom may be professional librarians elsewhere.

A theological library with *single-tradition* constituency would be mainly identified with a single religious denomination or movement. The educational institution typically offers liberal arts or professional education for members of the denomination as well as specialized training for religious professionals in that tradition. A variation on this pattern occurs when the institution identifies with a religious movement such as Pentecostalism or Evangelicalism rather than with a denomination per se. The users of these libraries are likely to be professors, students of the ministry, alumni, and local clergy. Although the population may be international, the cohesive factor is the common tradition. A Roman Catholic seminary that prepares priests for the church would be one example of the single-tradition type. Bible colleges and denominational universities are often of this type. Single-tradition institutions may vary in the degree to which their faculty or students are drawn from the tradition. Some single-tradition institutions operate at the graduate level. Many of these institutions in North America are accredited by the Association of Theological Schools in the United States and Canada. Libraries of this type usually have one or more professional librarians.

A theological library with a *multiple-tradition* constituency operates in an ecumenical educational institution providing graduate education for persons seeking ordination in several traditions. Another example occurs when seminaries or schools of various traditions share a consortial collection representing a variety of faith traditions, each educating its own religious workers and scholars, sometimes on separate campuses near a centralized library. Users of libraries of this type are also likely to be professors, students, alumni, and local clergy. The supporting institutions often seek accreditation from ATS or similar national bodies worldwide. The staff of multiple-tradition libraries are also likely to include one or more professionals.

Finally, a theological library might have an *extra-traditional* context when its sponsoring institution, such as a secular university offering graduate degrees in religious studies, emphasizes the scholarship of religions as human cultural phenomena rather than the preparation of religious adherents for ministerial work. Users of these libraries are professors, students, and scholars worldwide. Such libraries often assemble large international collections in a wide variety of disciplines and media, such as sociology of religion, history, linguistics, anthropology, archaeology, ethics, philosophy, literature, and the arts. These collections concerning the cultural record inform the program in religious studies. In large libraries associated with research universities, there will be many professional librarians, one of whom is designated the religion specialist who selects resources and assists readers with inquiries in religious studies.

In the third place, theological libraries, especially of the single-tradition or multiple-tradition type, participate not only in the information of students, but in their spiritual formation for religious work. The library accomplishes this through an ethos of hospitality, not only in its intellectual openness to collecting a wide variety of points of view, but in the librarians' respect for the students' freedom of inquiry. The library building provides quiet spaces not only for reading but also for contemplation, worship, and prayer. The library often provides spaces for group discussion and events that stimulate it. Exhibits of archives and artifacts call attention to the spiritual heritage of the institution, especially during anniversary or memorial occasions. Like many faculty members in small institutions, librarians may be called on to provide spiritual support to students in moments of intellectual and personal crisis. Since many theological librarians also hold advanced degrees in a theological discipline, they may also serve on thesis committees or occasionally teach courses.

In the fourth place, theological libraries respond creatively to changes in their religious communities, including technological innovations in information and religious education, changes in religious populations and publishing patterns worldwide, and threats to religious freedom in turbulent political situations. Advances in technology demand that libraries not only keep up with developments in hardware, systems, and metadata, but that they rebalance their acquisitions to supply more electronic resources as their schools shift to online instruction. While denominational populations and related seminary populations in the Northern Hemisphere are diminishing, the global South is experiencing significant denominational growth with consequent demands for theological education and for production of scholarly publications in relevant languages. Theological libraries worldwide collect scholarly materials by and about growing religious communities and find ways to facilitate their institutions' scholarly conversation on a global scale. Theological libraries anchor a global perspective on intellectual freedom that can assist their faculty, students, and institutions to resist the challenges to scholarship and community that economic and political tensions present worldwide. The energy for these efforts comes from hospitality, that powerful engine of respect and appreciation for the value of others' lives and for open dialogue with their perspectives on the divine. Theological libraries host intellectual inquiry because inquiry is an act of faith. They resource, harvest, steward, and disseminate the responses made by scholars, proponents, critics, and students to the claims of their faith traditions. Theological libraries value the accumulated wisdom of the ages, but they remember that a single voice may cry in the wilderness, speak under a tree, or sing in the courts of kings.

## Works Cited

Trotti, John B. (2002). "The Theological Library: In Touch With the Witnesses." In *Christian Librarianship: Essays On The Integration of Faith and Profession,* edited by Gregory A. Smith, 48–54. Jefferson, NC: Macfarland. Originally given as an address at the dedication of the Cook Center for Theological Research at Western Theological Seminary and published in *Reformed Review* 35 (Spring 1982): 157–61.

## Further Reading

### Collections and Periodicals

Graham, M. Patrick, Valerie R. Hotchkiss, and Kenneth E. Row, eds. 1996. *The American Theological Library Association: Essays In Celebration of the First Fifty Years*. Evanston, IL: ATLA.

McMahon, Melody Layton and David R. Stewart, eds. 2006. *A Broadening Conversation: Classic Readings in Theological Librarianship*. Lanham, MD: The Scarecrow Press.

Smith, Gregory A., ed. 2002. *Christian Librarianship: Essays On The Integration of Faith and Profession*. Jefferson, NC: McFarland.

*Theological Education* 40, no. 1 (2004).

*Theological Librarianship: An Online Journal of the American Theological Library Association*.

Trott, Garrett B. 2019. *The Faithful Librarian: Essays on Christianity in the Profession*. Jefferson, NC: McFarland.

### Individual Items

Allison, W. H. 1908-1912. "Theological Libraries." In *The New Schaff-Herzog Encyclopedia of Religious Knowledge*, edited by Samuel Macauley Jackson, 336–41. New York: Funk & Wagnalls.

Bidlack, Beth. 2006. "Some Observations on Theological Librarianship in Seminary and University Contexts." *ATLA Summary of Proceedings* 60: 38–48.

Bollier, John A. 2006. "Introduction" to Part 5. In *A Broadening Conversation: Classic Readings in Theological Librarianship*, edited by Melody Layton McMahon and David R. Stewart, 233–6. Lanham, MD: The Scarecrow Press.

Bramah, Michael. 2006. "Introduction" to Part 4. In *A Broadening Conversation: Classic Readings in Theological Librarianship*, edited by Melody Layton McMahon and David R. Stewart, 177–9. Lanham, MD: The Scarecrow Press.

Clarence, Judy. 2004. "ATLA and World Religions." *ATLA Summary of Proceedings* 58: 80–2.

Clark, J. W. 1968. *Libraries in The Medieval and Renaissance Periods*. The Rede Lecture, 1894. Chicago: Argonaut, Inc.

Coalter, Milton J. 1999. "Remarks Not Previously Given on a Discipline Too Little in Evidence." *Atla Summary of Proceedings* 53: 112 ff.

Corcoran, Monica. 2006. "Introduction" to Part 2. In *A Broadening Conversation: Classic Readings in Theological Librarianship*, edited by Melody Layton McMahon and David R. Stewart, 55–8. Lanham, MD: The Scarecrow Press.

Crawford, Eileen. 2006. "Introduction" to Part 6. In *A Broadening Conversation: Classic Readings in Theological Librarianship,* edited by Melody Layton McMahon and David R. Stewart, 271-4. Lanham, MD: The Scarecrow Press.

Crow, Paul A. 1966. "Professors and Librarians: Partners in the Oikumené." In *ATLA Summary of Proceedings* 20: 71-6.

Cuninggim, Merrimon. 1954. "The Seminary Library From The Faculty Point of View." *ATLA Summary of Proceedings* 8: 22 ff.

Daly, Simeon. 1990. "That They All May Be One." *ATLA Summary of Proceedings* 44: 216 ff.

Dare, Philip N. 1994. "Theological Libraries." In *Encyclopedia of Library History,* edited by Wayne A. Wiegand and Donald M. David, Jr., 621-3. New York: Garland.

Davis, Donald G., Jr. 2002. "Intellectual Freedom and Evangelical Faith." In *Christian Librarianship: Essays On The Integration of Faith and Profession,* edited by Gregory A. Smith, 131-8. Jefferson, NC: Mcfarland.

Davis, Donald G., Jr. and John Mark Tucker. 2002. "The Master We Serve: The Call of The Christian Librarian To The Secular Workplace." In *Christian Librarianship: Essays On The Integration of Faith and Profession,* edited by Gregory A. Smith, 40-7. Jefferson, NC: Mcfarland.

Dempsey, Mary A. 1999. "Serving The Religion Information Needs of The Public." *Atla Summary of Proceedings* 53: 219 ff.

Dickerson, G. Fay and John A. Peltz. 1974. "The Index to Religious Periodical Literature: Past, Present and Future." In *ATLA Summary of Proceedings* 28: 87 ff.

Doty, Philip, Duane Harbin, and Sandra E. Riggs. 2003. "Theological Librarians as Copyright Leaders." *ATLA Summary of Proceedings* 57: 63-81.

Dunkly, James. 1991. "Theological Libraries and Theological Librarians in Theological Education." *ATLA Summary of Proceedings* 45: 227 ff.

———. 1992. "Some Values in Theological Librarianship." *ATLA Summary of Proceedings* 46: 193 ff.

Ebertz, Susan, Carrie Hackney, and Ann Hotta. 2005. "Encouraging Diversity: Cultural and Ethnic Issues Facing Theological Students of Color as They Use the Library." *ATLA Summary of Proceedings* 59: 123-41.

Elliott, L. R. 1949. "Seminary Libraries and Theological Education." *ATLA Summary of Proceedings* 2: C1-C9.

———. 1953. "'Hitherto': Six Years of ATLA." *ATLA Summary of Proceedings* 7: 1 ff.

Gunn, Shirley, Cindy Lu, Mayra Picos-Lee, D'Anna Shotts, Margaret Tarpley, and Mariel Deluca Voth. 2005. "Cultural Competency in the Theological Library." *ATLA Summary of Proceedings* 59: 18-26.

Hamm, G. Paul. 1979. "A Look at the Past." *ATLA Summary of Proceedings* 33: 93 ff.

Jones, Arthur E. 1960. "Some Thoughts on the Joint Theological School–Liberal Arts College Library." *ATLA Summary of Proceedings* 14: 85 ff.

Kortendick, James J. 1965. "The Theological Librarian: His Commitment and Strategy." *ATLA Summary of Proceedings* 19: 105 ff.

Krieger, Alan D. 1996. "From the Outside In: A History of Roman Catholic Participation in the ATLA." In *The American Theological Library Association: Essays In Celebration of The First Fifty Years*, edited by M. Patrick Graham, Valerie R. Hotchkiss, and Kenneth E. Row, 36–42. Evanston, IL: ATLA.

Lincoln, Timothy D. 2004. "What's a Seminary Library For?" *Theological Education* 40, no. 1: 1-10.

Loyd, Roger L. 2006. "Introduction" to Part 3. In *A Broadening Conversation: Classic Readings in Theological Librarianship*, edited by Melody Layton McMahon and David R. Stewart, 125–8. Lanham, MD: The Scarecrow Press.

McMahon, Melody Layton. 2010. "Theological Librarianship: An Unapologetic Apology." *Theological Librarianship* 3, no. 1 (June): 7–14.

———. 2004. "Librarians and Teaching Faculty in Collaboration: New Incentives, New Opportunities." *Theological Education* 40, no. 1: 73–88.

Morris, Raymond P. 1953. "Theological Librarianship as a Ministry." *Atla Summary of Proceedings* 7: 31 ff.

Newhall, Janet E. 1954. "The Library Staff Views the Library Program." *Atla Summary of Proceedings* 8: 22 ff.

O'Brien, Elmer J. and Betty A. O'Brien. 1996. "From Volunteerism to Corporate Professionalism: A Historical Sketch of the American Theological Library Association." In *The American Theological Library Association: Essays In Celebration of The First Fifty Years*, edited by M. Patrick Graham, Valerie R. Hotchkiss, and Kenneth E. Row, 3–24. Evanston, IL: ATLA.

Pacala, Leon. 1981. "Theological Libraries Revisited." *ATLA Summary of Proceedings* 35: 1 ff.

Paulus, Michael J, Jr. 2006. "Spiritual Culture and the Theological Library: The Role of the Princeton Theological Seminary Library in the Religious Life of Theological Students in the Nineteenth Century." *ATLA Summary of Proceedings* 60: 220-8.

Peterson, Herman. 2001. "Theological Librarianship as Ministry." *ATLA Summary of Proceedings* 55: 231-50.

Roberts, Walter N. 1954. "The Library From The Point of View of The Administration." In *ATLA Summary of Proceedings* 8: 22 ff.

Rockwell, William. 1943–44. "Theological Libraries in the United States." *Religion In Life* 13: 545–55.

Schreiter, Robert J. 1990. "Globalization and Theological Libraries." *ATLA Summary of Proceedings* 44: 146–59.

Schrodt, Paul. 1996. "Theological Librarianship and Theological Education." In *The American Theological Library Association: Essays In Celebration of The First Fifty Years*, edited by M. Patrick Graham, Valerie R. Hotchkiss, and Kenneth E. Row, 133–49. Evanston, IL: ATLA.

Schultz, Susan. 1961. "Remarks on Women in Theological Librarianship." *ATLA Summary of Proceedings* 15: 100 ff.

Selinger, Suzanne. 2004. "ATLA and the Religions of the United States and Canada." *ATLA Summary of Proceedings* 58: 76–9.

Sherrill, Lewis J. 1948. "Seminary Librarians (Greetings and Challenge From ATS)." *ATLA Summary of Proceedings* 1: 2 ff.

Skreslet, Paula. 2008. "Basic Primary Sources in Islamic Religion." *Theological Librarianship: An Online Journal of the American Theological Library Association* 1, no. 1 (3 June).

Smalley, Martha Lund and Paul F. Stuehrenberg. 2004. "Incorporating Global Perspectives into Theological Education: The Role of the Library." *Theological Education* 40, no. 1: 59–72.

Stewart, David R. 2000. "Libraries, Western Christian." In *Encyclopedia of Monasticism*, edited by Wm. M. Johnston, 235–6. Vol. 1. Chicago: Fitzroy Dearborn.

Stokes, Roy. 1993. "Shadow and Substance." *ATLA Summary of Proceedings* 47: 196 ff.

Stuehrenberg, Paul F. 2005. "Presidential Address: Who Will Advocate for the Theological Library?" *ATLA Summary of Proceedings* 59: 29–32.

Tait, Jennifer Woodruff. 2004. "True and Capable Heirs: A Survey of Resources on the African Methodist Episcopal Church." *ATLA Summary of Proceedings* 58: 183–95.

Tarpley, Margaret, Shirley Gunn, and D'Anna Shotts. 2004. "International, Cultural, and Ethnic Issues for Theological Librarians." *ATLA Summary of Proceedings* 58: 168–73.

Tarpley, Margaret. 2008. "The U.S. as a Foreign Culture: Helping International Students, Faculty, and Staff Navigate the American Cultural Landscape." *ATLA Summary of Proceedings* 62: 324–8.

Taylor, Sharon. 2002. "Power and Responsibility: Reflections on Theological Librarianship." *ATLA Summary of Proceedings* 56: 51 ff.

Treat, James. 2004. "Native Religious Activism in the Red Power Era." *ATLA Summary of Proceedings* 58: 41–9.

Trotti, John B. 2002. "The Theological Library: In Touch With the Witnesses." In *Christian Librarianship: Essays On The Integration of Faith and Profession,* edited by Gregory A. Smith, 48–54. Jefferson, NC: Macfarland.

Uhrich, Helen B. 1957. "The Community of Learning." *ATLA Summary of Proceedings* 11: 1–6.

Weigel, Gustave. 1961. "When Catholic and Protestant Theologies Meet." *ATLA Summary of Proceedings* 15: 60 ff.

Welch, Claude. 1987. "The Theological Library: Servant or Partner." *ATLA Summary of Proceedings* 41: 156 ff.

White, Ernest. 1986. "A Combined Greeting to ATLA Number 40 and Reflection on ATLA Number 1." *ATLA Summary of Proceedings* 40: 172 ff.

Womack, Anne Richardson. 2006. "Introduction" to Part 1. In *A Broadening Conversation: Classic Readings in Theological Librarianship,* edited Melody Layton McMahon and David R. Stewart, 3–6. Lanham, MD: The Scarecrow Press.

# CHAPTER 2

# Theological Librarianship as a Career Path

KELLY CAMPBELL AND ANDREW KECK

## Introduction

The career path to theological librarianship is circuitous. Most theological librarians emerge from a career journey containing a variety of positions and roles in ministry, libraries, or higher education. In addition to various roles or careers, the educational preparation of theological librarians can vary. In this chapter, we will draw upon the literature of theological librarianship to help answer the following questions. What are theological librarians? Is theological librarianship a ministry or an occupation? What specific experiences or education are valued components to be a theological librarian? After reading this chapter, you will learn the common pathways to developing into and having a career in theological librarianship.

## What are Theological Librarians?

As we begin to explore theological librarianship as a career path, the first step is to answer the question of what a theological librarian is. In reviewing the library literature from 1924 to 1994, the literature contains fewer than sixty-five articles or citations on the topic of theological libraries or librarians (Karp and Keck 1996a). However, the literature notes two general definitions of theological librarians. These two general definitions are analogous to two sides of a coin and continue to provide both tension and balance for theological librarians. The first literature definition is of theological librarians as "people performing ministry" (p. 35). Some theological librarians define themselves as ministers and as being in the ministry of helping students and faculty. The second literature definition is of theological librarians as "people who provide linkages among theology, church, scholarship, education, diverse constituencies, and both scholarly and popular literature" (p. 35). Both definitions make the general assumption that a theological librarian is a librarian working in a theological or religious setting or a librarian supporting an organization in the field of theology or religion. The question of ministry or occupation will be explored further below.

Settings for theological librarians can be quite varied. When one expands the settings to include "linkages" among theology, church, and scholarly and popular literature, the settings become inclusive of many scholarly, educational, religious, and community networks. While the typical theological librarian might work in a seminary setting, there are various additional settings containing works which can be theological or religious in nature. These various settings include denominational libraries, universities or colleges with religious departments or degrees, archival libraries documenting religious or theological history and movements, as well as community and even national libraries. For example, a theological librarian works at the United States Library of Congress overseeing theological and religious subjects. Therefore, in the broadest sense, a theological librarian is a librarian providing library services within contexts holding the materials of and about religious and theological traditions.

While theological librarians work in different contexts, they also fulfill different roles or positions within and throughout institutions. Theological librarians work as subject specialists, cataloging librarians, library directors, instructional designers, educational technologists, research assistants, copyright specialists, digital humanities librarians, scholarly communication coordinators, event planners, and many other titles. Theological librarians' various titles speak to the broad and integrated importance of the library and information sciences. Historically, information was limited to print and archives materials; however, with the rapid increase and accessibility of information, theological librarians can utilize their organizational and information skills in an ever-increasing variety of positions. Theological librarians, with their skill sets and competencies, are valuable to institutions beyond the library and its traditional positions.

Beyond these various contexts and roles, theological librarians serve as partners in the educational process. The educational process can be narrowly defined as students in a seminary setting and broadly expanded to include clientele visiting a denominational repository. Theological librarians not only provide collections and policies; they educate people. They teach persons how to find the information they are seeking or help an individual understand the various sources of information available. As an example, librarians working as instructional designers help faculty design their online courses and are experts in various pedagogies. Throughout their various roles, theological librarians are partners in the educational process and many theological librarians were drawn to the career largely due to the educational component.

Based on who theological librarians are, many in the profession would define theological librarians as a tribe. With a wide variety of pathways into the profession and diverse experiences and credentials, the tribe of theological librarians is open and accepting. Theological librarians serving beyond traditional libraries would self-identify as a part of the tribe; while others without experience or credentials serving in theological library roles would claim their place in the tribe. The rationale for the word "tribe" emerges from the theological and religious arena where denominations and faith traditions tend to be tribal. The beauty of the theological librarian's tribe is that our work is what joins us together not the contrasting and differing beliefs. In this tribe, members can work cooperatively together to support information and library resources while holding drastically differing beliefs and faith traditions. Working cooperatively to build collections, educate clientele (faculty, students, etc.), and preserve resources and materials for the future generate the work that brings various theological librarians and libraries together.

Due to the circuitous route, theological librarians come from a variety of backgrounds. Each theological librarian's pathway is unique and normally takes several twists and turns before settling into the field of theological librarianship. Before entering careers in the field, many theological librarians have had some prior engagement with a theological library, usually as a student or patron. A challenge for diverse recruitment into the profession is to reach those who desire to work in libraries but who are unfamiliar with theological libraries.

# Theological Librarianship as a Ministry or Occupation

Theological librarianship can be a ministry but is not universally observed as such (Karp and Keck 1996b; Keck 1996). Some practitioners will make the case explicitly with formal and informal endorsements by their faith tradition (in some cases, including ordination). Others will view their work primarily as an occupation or profession without any explicit reference to considerations of faith or ministry. Many will frame theological librarianship with both categories, identifying aspects of their roles and work that primarily fit as ministry or occupation.

A number of factors can lead to a consideration of theological librarianship as a ministry:

- engagement in work that is explicitly service oriented (such as reference assistance),
- working with patrons (clientele) who are engaged in and/or preparing for ministry,
- working with colleagues in the library or within the broader organization who view their work as ministry,
- working within a broader organization with specific religious commitments and/or understandings of ministry,
- viewing the library collections as representing special religious knowledge and/or collective witness of prior adherents,
- approaching theological librarianship as a personal calling into ministry.

Many of these are contextual to the specific library and work demands. A person employed within a context of preparing students for ministry is perhaps more likely to also see their own work within this framework. Institutions with their own deep religious commitments could inform how individuals employed within the institution may view their work. These factors are by no means determinative. A librarian may maintain an independent view of their work regardless of the clientele and institutional commitments. A librarian may have different religious commitments than their employing institution or no commitments at all.

Other factors considered above are more specific to the individual librarian in terms of how they come into the profession and view their own work. Theological librarians who enter the profession from discerning their own call to ministry may be more likely to find theological librarianship as a ministry. In other words, if one is prepared to see theological librarianship as a ministry, one is more likely to see it as such. Viewpoints can also change over time, especially when additional factors noted above may be at play. A theological librarian may initially see their work as an occupation and then develop an appreciation for it as a ministry as part of engaging with a ministry-focused organization and their clientele.

When considered as an occupation, the contexts for theological librarians vary globally as do the requirements and process for hire. In the United States, for instance, the Master of Library Science (or equivalent) from an ALA-accredited graduate program is normative. Hiring is done through formal search processes, often national in scope, in order to identify and hire the best librarian for a given position. Theological librarians, as a subspecialty of academic librarians, can be expected to have completed further graduate work in theology or religion in addition to the Master of Library Science. While not universally true, this is especially true for library directors and those who work in collection development or reference.

Theological librarianship as ministry or occupation are not mutually exclusive perspectives and can be held simultaneously. Even if one believes theological librarianship to be primarily a ministry, the work can also be an occupation requiring specialized skills, education, and/or experience. In some places, librarians receive similar or parallel status as faculty with nomenclature referring to "library faculty," tenure or tenure-like provisions, and formal ranks. Similarly, even if one believes theological librarianship to be primarily an occupation, working with materials, people, and institutions with religious commitments can affect the context of one's work and how it may be viewed.

## Education and Experience for Theological Librarianship

In the United States higher education system, the Master of Library Science (MLS) degree is largely viewed as the credential connected to the title "librarian." Plenty of people work in libraries without an MLS degree, but the title "librarian" is often reserved for employees with the requisite master's degree and is sometimes accompanied with a distinct set of benefits and responsibilities. Exceptions abound and this precise connection between degree, title, and benefits/responsibilities continues to be questioned by libraries where traditional "librarians" work alongside a growing number of other qualified professionals who happen to lack a Master of Library Science degree, or who possess other master's degrees in fields such as education or technology.

As noted above, the Master of Library Science degree is not always required for every position within the library. Some positions can be classified as paraprofessional and other library positions are classified as professional but require expertise and education focused in other specialized areas (such as information technology, data management, accounting, etc.). Finally, there are individuals who achieve typical librarian positions by virtue of "equivalent experience" in libraries that is deemed to take the place of a formal degree.

The director or head librarian at a seminary library can be a special case in theological librarianship in the United States. Within the Association of Theological Schools' *Standards of Accreditation*, the chief library administrator "ordinarily" is a voting member of the faculty and "normally" possesses graduate degrees in library science and in theological studies. While these standards set norms, there is nothing to prevent a school from appointing someone without these educational credentials or to require further credentials (such as a PhD or EdD).

A survey conducted for non-US based theological librarians by the Theological Book Network (shared privately with the authors) revealed that slightly fewer than half of those responding noted a head librarian with a degree in library science. Of those with specialized degrees or education, slightly better than one-third of all respondents had degrees at the master's or doctoral level. As further responses indicated, there was great interest in further education and training in library science but limited opportunities in some parts of the world.

Within a degree or educational program, "library science" is a broad category covering the breadth of what librarians and libraries may be called upon to know and do. Topics can include library management, collection development, reference, cataloging, circulation, archives, digital resources, digitization, scholarly communication, information literacy, library instruction, library marketing, etc. Many library science programs in the United States also engage in information science, which may include database management, information architecture, data mining, programming, multimedia, and artificial intelligence. Although the American Library Association provides some standards as part of the accreditation of programs, individual information or library schools determine the precise learning outcomes and curriculum for the degree, and so there can be variation between schools and graduates regarding particular knowledge and competencies. Ongoing paradigmatic changes in libraries, scholarly communication, and higher education make lifelong learning beyond the degree essential for the modern librarian.

Experience desired or required for theological librarians involves technical competencies (see Johnson, Graham, Berryhill, and Keck 2012), subject knowledge competencies, and cultural competencies. Technical competencies can include mastery of cataloging and metadata practices, information literacy and research skills, electronic resource management, etc. These are helpful in designing general library operations and performing specific library tasks. Subject knowledge competencies include the various areas of theological inquiry and knowledge. These competencies are essential for cataloging as well as for providing reference assistance and instruction. Finally, cultural competencies relate to the diverse set of library clientele and a broader set of colleagues within theological education. These can be related to a set of soft skills that allow one to connect to various cultures and clientele of most theological libraries: faculty, administrators, master's students, doctoral students, local pastors, and community patrons. Experience is particularly essential for the cultural competencies and certainly can advance, if not partially substitute for, formal education and training.

# Conclusion: The Road to Theological Librarianship

A great conversation-starter among theological librarians is to ask how they came to the profession and the particular position they occupy. Each response is unique, but some common pathways can be discerned. At least four entry points can be discerned.

First, some librarians enter the theological library field possessing both formal theological training and a library science degree with their intent to work in a seminary, theological school, or religious library setting for their entire career. Many of these individuals feel that theological librarianship is a calling or ministry.

Second, librarians complete their PhD in theology or religious studies planning to become a professor, researcher, or lecturer; however, they cannot find a faculty position and find themselves in the library where they can utilize their subject expertise and teaching skills. Typically, these individuals find that the gifts of helping and working with students and faculty nicely complement their desire to have a career working in higher education. The literature supports this entry point into theological librarianship as Andrew Keck surveyed 371 American members of Atla (founded in 1946 as the American Theological Library Association) and found that many saw their work as 'parallel' to the theology professors. He notes Connolly C. Gamble Jr.'s 1962 presentation to Atla (Gamble 2006) that argued for the library as a "central teaching agency of the seminary rather than a mere warehouse for book storage."

Third, other theological librarians come to the field from broader academic librarianship. In some cases, they may work in a university setting as the religious or humanities librarian, serving as the primary connection between religious and theological faculty and library services.

Fourth, others enter the theological library field after working in the secular or business field and find themselves going back to school seeking to contribute back and to find value in their work. Thus, these individuals find the career of theological librarianship as a second career after their first.

The career path to theological librarianship is as varied as the contexts where theological librarians are employed, the precise work one is called upon to do, the professional and ministerial meaning ascribed to such work, and the preparations to do such work. This pathway to theological librarianship can be found globally; however, what ties theological librarianship together is a focus upon serving a diverse clientele interested and curious about religious traditions and studies accessed, documented, and preserved by libraries and archives. If a person is interested in a career in theological librarianship, the pathway is open.

## Works Cited

Gamble, Connolly C., Jr. 2006. "Contemporary Challenges to Theological Librarianship." In *A Broadening Conversation: Classic Readings in Theological Librarianship*, edited by Melody Layton McMahon and David R. Stewart. Lanham, Maryland: The Scarecrow Press.

Johnson, Tammy, M. Patrick Graham, Carisse Mickey Berryhill, and Andrew J. Keck. 2012. "Core Competencies for Theological Librarians Panel." *ATLA Summary of Proceedings* 66: 223–31.

Karp, Rashelle S. and Andrew J. Keck. 1996a. "Theological Librarianship: Toward a Profile of a Profession." *College & Research Libraries* 57, no. 1: 35–42. *https://doi.org/10.5860/crl_57_01_35*.

———. "Theological Librarianship." 1996b. In *American Theological Library Association: Essays in Celebration of the First Fifty Years*, edited by M. Patrick Graham, Valerie R. Hotchkiss, and Kenneth E. Row, 172–82. Evanston, IL: ATLA. *https://books.atla.com/index.php/atlapress/catalog/book/6*.

Keck, Andrew J. 1996. "Information or Divine Access: Theological Librarianship within the Context of a Ministry." In *American Theological Library Association: Essays in Celebration of the First Fifty Years*, edited by M. Patrick Graham, Valerie R. Hotchkiss, and Kenneth E. Row, 172–82. Evanston, IL: ATLA.

## Additional Resources

Peterson, Herman A. 2001. "Theological Librarianship as a Ministry." *ATLA Summary of Proceedings* 55: 231–50.

Shaffett, John E. 2013. "Theological Librarianship as a Ministry." *ATLA Summary of Proceedings* 67: 69–83.

Smith, Gregory A., ed. 2002. *Christian Librarianship: Essays on the Integration of Faith and Profession*. Jefferson, NC: McFarland.

*Introduction to Theological Libraries*

# *Theological Libraries Worldwide*

# CHAPTER 3

# Christian Theological Libraries in Africa

EPHRAIM MUDAVE

## Introduction

This chapter outlines the brief historical development of theological libraries in Africa, of predominantly Christian Evangelical background, the current state, and future trends. Included are libraries of theology departments, faculties or institutes of theology, and academic libraries whose collection includes significant holdings of resources relevant for theological and religious studies. Areas of focus include human resources, library collections, application of information and communication technology (ICT), and the role of library associations and other supporting organizations. The chapter highlights some challenges and opportunities faced by theological libraries and librarians on the continent and the anticipated trends.

## History and Development

The development of theological libraries and librarianship in Africa has been historically uneven, showing huge differences pitting francophone against anglophone regions (Bowers 1989). This situation does not seem to have changed much. Even within a given region, there exist huge disparities in terms of the number and quality of information resources, trained library staff, physical library buildings, and use of technology, with the anglophone region having better-equipped libraries. These disparities are historical, depicting a direct

Image 1: Tony Wilmot Library of the Africa International University in Nairobi, Kenya. ©AIU

relationship with the activities of the white missionaries who introduced Christianity to the continent. Generally, theological schools and Christian universities in Africa were established by churches or Christian mission boards. They mostly began as centers to train church ministers. Eventually, they developed into theological schools and universities.

The Association for Christian Theological Education in Africa (ACTEA)[1] lists four accredited post-graduate institutions, fourteen post-secondary, seven candidate, and eleven affiliates as evangelical theological training institutions. However, the number of theological schools of various sizes is not registered with ACTEA and the number could run into hundreds. Others include Adventist institutions that have over twenty universities and colleges and over forty Catholic seminaries ranging from minor to major schools. Historically, Neill (1964) mentions Fourah Bay College in Sierra Leone, founded in 1827, as the oldest theological college in Africa. Among the first theological libraries in East Africa is Uganda Christian University in the Bishop Tucker Theological College, founded in 1913 to train the Church of Uganda leaders.

A survey was carried out in February 2019 that sought to establish the status of theological libraries in Africa (Mudave n.d.). The goal of the survey was representation of the population and not a high response rate. Contacts for the institutions were taken from the ACTEA directory and internet searches under "theological institutions in Africa," "Catholic seminaries in Africa," and "Adventist colleges in Africa." A total of ninety schools formed the population. This included university, college, and seminary libraries across all denominations. A census approach was adopted with questionnaires sent to listed contacts of all the schools. The Lime survey tool was used to send the questionnaires and analyze the responses. Twenty addresses were invalid or the individuals had left the institutions being surveyed. Three follow-up reminder emails were sent but, at the end of the month, only sixteen librarians had responded to the questionnaires. Although the response rate was low, it met the goal of the survey as there were two responses from francophone countries and all regions were represented, except the north.

Most of the libraries surveyed (10 out of 16) were more than 30 years old. Despite the number of years that theological libraries have existed in Africa, their development has been very slow. It is worth noting that more than half of those surveyed (56.25%) existed in stand-alone purpose-built library buildings while the rest (43.75%) were attached to other buildings. Whereas space was a constraint in libraries that were part of other buildings, those purpose-built enjoyed not only space but also the ambiance that made them attractive to users.

## Collection Development

In developing their collections, gifts play a substantial part in all theological libraries. The dwindling budgets imply fewer funds are available for the purchase of resources. However small, most libraries indicated that they spent the little they had on books. Without proper weeding policies, most libraries end up with collections they do not need. As of February 28, 2019, six libraries (37.5%) had over 30,000 volumes on theology or theology-related areas, followed by five libraries (31.25%) having between 10,000 and 20,000 volumes. Only three libraries had less than 10,000 volumes, with one having between 2,000 and 5,000 volumes. None had less than 2,000 volumes. It is therefore noteworthy that more than half of the libraries surveyed had more than 10,000 theology and theology-related volumes.

Most of the collections in theological libraries consist predominantly of books in English, with a few in French and local languages. Of the academic journal titles, only a few libraries in large schools subscribe to accredited print titles in theology. Due to the high cost of academic journals, most libraries have broken-run back issues that mostly were received as donations or on complimentary arrangements. The majority (10 out of 16) of schools surveyed had subscribed to electronic journal databases either directly or through consortia. Popular databases included EbscoHost, Atlas, EBSCO Religion and Theology, JSTOR, and EBSCO Academic Search Elite. In general, access to relevant academic journals is a challenge for theological libraries.

In organizing their collections most libraries use the Dewey Decimal Classification System while the rest use the Library of Congress System. In some countries, the government determines the classification system through the accrediting agencies. For example, Kenyan universities are required by the Commission for University Education to use the Library of Congress classification system and the second edition of the Anglo-American Cataloguing Rules before they are accredited.

It should be noted that the quality and quantity of theological library collections greatly depend on the lecturers who recommend books for purchase. Therefore, the level of training and exposure of the lecturers and, subsequently, the librarians becomes critical for collection development.

## Automation and ICT Infrastructure

Uptake of automation and ICT infrastructure, which started at major African academic libraries in the 1990s, has been low compared to other world regions. In the survey conducted in 2019, most libraries (68.75%) were automated, with half of them being fully automated. However, it was observed that four libraries did not have automation software and did not respond to the question when asked whether they had computers in the library or not. However, most libraries, even those that were not automated, would typically have a stand-alone computer or two for the library staff.

Apart from one, all the respondents had an internet connection in their library–an indication that connectivity has greatly increased in recent years. However, fast, affordable and reliable access is still a challenge. The situation is fast-changing, with many countries now gaining broadband access and increased access through mobile phones. According to the 2019 report of the Miniwatts Marketing Group, the 58 African countries had an average internet penetration rate of 36% of their total population. In individual countries, 26 out of 58 countries had an internet penetration rate of above 30% of their populations. The total number of internet users rose from 4,534,400 in 2000 to 474,120,563 by March 30,2019 (Miniwatts Marketing Group 2019). Fiber optics have crisscrossed the continent and connected Africa to the rest of the world through undersea cables, giving hope for increased global data communication. This is a call to theological librarians to take advantage and prepare to serve users using the internet and associated technologies because library services are needed beyond the walls of the library building.

## Staffing

The total number of libraries sampled when writing this chapter was sixteen, and for such a number to have only 25 librarians indicates that most have only one or two staff members. Almost half of the staff (11) were permanently employed, while the rest were either on a short contract or volunteer terms. It is encouraging to note that no library reported lacking a trained librarian. Most librarians had a bachelor's degree, while the second-greatest number held diplomas (2-year certification below the bachelor's degree). There were also those with a master's degree, and two had doctoral degrees. A few more were trained at certificate levels. However, only two had done some (2-year) training that included aspects of theological librarianship, while the rest had done only general librarianship training. Even the term *theological librarianship* was new to almost all librarians, with only one aware of an available opportunity for training. These figures indicate that most theological libraries are understaffed, with some being run by librarians who have not been properly trained. It is common to find former students of theology running libraries in Africa, especially in small denominational libraries.

All basic library services are being offered in almost all theological libraries, including circulation of materials, cataloguing, current awareness, reference, SDI, interlibrary loan, and preservation services.

## Information Literacy (IL)

Competent and lifelong learners are made. Information literacy (IL) is key to ensuring that lifelong learning skills are inculcated in students. Most libraries offer orientation sessions to all first-year students and follow with user education in various formats. Only one library had an IL course as a formal unit of instruction, with three having it as part of a credit unit. Librarians generally taught the IL component, even when it was part of another unit. The librarians taught and assessed the students, with their grades in the IL component counting for the overall score in the unit. The level of training of the librarians determines their understanding and involvement in information literacy initiatives. Therefore, libraries that lack adequately trained staff are not able to offer the programme effectively.

# Library Associations and Other Supporting Organizations

Library associations are key to the professional exchange of ideas and development in the profession. In Africa, most libraries belong to one or more of the existing national, regional, or interest group library associations. They include the Christian Association of Librarians in Africa-Kenya (CALA-K), Malawi Library and Information Consortium, Kenya Library Association (KLA), and the Library and Information Association of South Africa (LIASA), among others. All of these associations organize workshops, conferences, and general meetings aimed at enhancing professionalism in librarianship and awareness of trends in the profession.

## Christian Association of Librarians in Africa (CALA)

Among these, CALA has been on the forefront in championing theological librarianship for over fifteen years. The association started as a parallel meeting alongside the principals and academic deans of theological colleges in Kenya under the name Nairobi Fellowship of Theological Colleges (NFTC). In 2002 CALA reinvented itself into a professional association for theological librarians. With sponsorship from the Accrediting Council for Theological Education in Africa (ACTEA), CALA held several training workshops in 2002 and 2003 for librarians that had no library training but were working in theological libraries. The attendees came from several African countries. Under the leadership of Phyllis Masso, CALA championed the automation of theological libraries, mostly in East Africa.

CALA currently organizes annual conferences every July and two general meetings focused on developing librarians and librarianship in theological institutions. The annual conferences are four-day events while general meetings are one-day events. Membership is open to individual librarians working in both Christian and secular institutions. The majority of the institutional membership comprises Christian universities and colleges. CALA exists to empower Christian librarians through professional development, scholarship, and spiritual encouragement for service in higher education and society in Africa. CALA hopes to be a continental association with chapters in each country. So far, the conferences and meetings have attracted attendance from Kenya, Ethiopia, Uganda, Tanzania, Burundi, South Africa, Malawi, Zimbabwe, Côte d'Ivoire, Ghana, Chad, the Democratic Republic of the Congo, Zambia, and Burkina Faso. Apart from Kenya, the conferences have also been held in Uganda and Tanzania. The secretariat is at the International Leadership University in Nairobi, Kenya.

*Image 2: Attendees of the 2017 meeting of CALA in Uganda. ©CALA*

## Association for Christian Theological Education in Africa (ACTEA)

Since its inception in 1976, ACTEA has played a key role in the development of theological libraries in Africa in several ways. First, it provided theological librarians a forum for exchange of information for personal and institutional development through *ACTEA Librarians eNews*. Unfortunately, this publication had its last issue in September 2006. Second, ACTEA sponsored one- and two-week library training workshops for librarians in Nairobi, Kenya in 2002. Third, ACTEA has established clear standards and guidelines for setting up and running libraries in theological institutions, which have played a key role in the development of theological libraries in Africa. Unfortunately, many institutions do not comply with the standards of ACTEA in stocking their libraries. However, institutions that are accredited by ACTEA have met the standards prescribed. The accreditation process of theological institutions by ACTEA has, to a great extent, enhanced the development of theological libraries in Africa. It was through ACTEA's library development programme that many theological schools in Africa were introduced to the Open Africa Programme that ensured free access to African journals in JSTOR.

## Theological Book Network (TBN)

Founded in 2004, the Theological Book Network (TBN) continues to be one of the main suppliers for high-quality theological and related books for African theological libraries. They do this in close consultation with the receiving institutions to ensure only relevant resources are shipped. They also offer free access to several online digital resources to support theological training. Additionally, due to high internet costs and erratic electricity, TBN has provided hard drives loaded with theological resources under Creative Commons licenses for use while the receiving colleges work on establishing stable infrastructures.

## Network for African Congregational Theology (NetAct)

The Network for African Congregational Theology (NetAct) was started in the year 2000 in Kenya and brings together theological institutions in the Presbyterian and Reformed tradition in sub-Saharan Africa. It was not until its general meeting in 2017 that the NetAct Information Portal was established, bringing together librarians in member institutions to work on providing needed information resources to students and faculty. To deliver this mandate, several librarians from member institutions have been trained and resources identified as a starting point for supporting theological education with electronic resources. More librarian training sessions are planned for different regions of Africa, including the francophone regions that were not in the initial plans. This initiative provides a much needed forum for the exchange of ideas and resources among theological librarians in Africa to address cutting-edge challenges.

## Consortia

With the increasing costs of journal and eBook subscriptions, individual libraries are finding it difficult to provide all that their users need. This calls for a collaborative approach to achieving common objectives. Consortia are one key way that libraries are addressing the need. A case in point in Kenya is the Kenya Libraries and Information Services Consortium (KLISC), which most theological libraries are part of. For a comparatively small annual fee, member libraries can access key journal databases for theological studies, including the Atla Religion Database, Atla Serials, the Catholic Periodical and Literature Index, New Testament Abstracts, Old Testament Abstracts, the Religion and Philosophy Collection, and other leading multidisciplinary databases. In addition to the e-journals, the consortium also provides access to EBSCO eBooks and ProQuest Ebook Central where many theological books are available as full text.

In summary, library associations and related organizations have played a significant role in the development of theological libraries and librarianship in Africa. This includes, but is not limited to, the provision of opportunities for knowledge sharing and benchmarking during conferences and workshops, as well as provision and sharing of resources and development of skills.

## Challenges and Opportunities

Theological libraries of whatever size are alive to the fact that librarianship is changing and the need to adapt to these changing environments to remain relevant. Some of the forces of change are external while others are internal. Brenda Bailey-Hainer, in her address to theological librarians in Melbourne (2014), observed that, although theological and religious studies libraries had proved to be remarkably resilient over time, their future will be majorly shaped by trends in higher education, trends in theological education, and general trends in academic libraries. Africa is not exempted from the same challenges. For example, in the hope of achieving sustainability, theological colleges and universities in the last fifteen years in Kenya have opened new campuses without proper planning and have ended up shutting them after spending heavily on their establishment. Two classic examples in Kenya are the Catholic University of East Africa, which had to close two of her campuses, and the University of Eastern Africa, Baraton, which had to close four campuses in a period of one year. Since librarians are rarely involved in the initial stages of such moves, there is always a strain when library services are finally required.

### Online, Distance, and eLearning
The other trend in higher education that has affected theological education and cannot be avoided is the need to offer alternative delivery modes including online, distance, and eLearning to meet the needs of the church. Online and distance learning is an attempt to address the challenge of the high cost of residential training programs and the inadequacy of trained ministers for the church. Many churches cannot afford to have their pastors away on study leave because they often have no replacement. The library is expected to support the new modes of learning and finds itself inadequate, one reason being that librarians are never consulted during curriculum development processes. Librarians, therefore, are expected to be creative and flexible to respond to the changing nature of academic instruction and offer the needed library service.

### Funding
Most theological libraries in Africa seem to have been affected in the last couple of years by decreased donor funding to theological institutions. Most institutions relied heavily on sponsorship from the West and now find it very difficult to

manage with the reducing support. With the additional declining student numbers for theological training, it is becoming increasingly difficult to rely on tuition fees from students to cover basic running costs. As Blessings Amina Akporhonor observed in a study on Nigerian libraries' funding (2005), libraries have very small budgets and often receive far less funding than the percentage that is usually earmarked for them. The high cost of information resources makes it even harder to find the needed titles in most libraries. This affects both the purchase of current information resources and the hiring of qualified librarians. The economies of many African countries have slumped, leaving buying of books a luxury and only possible when extremely necessary.

In addition to institutions' efforts to market theology to increase student numbers, libraries need to seek alternative funding streams. Suggested alternatives would include creatively using available space–for example, providing available space for meetings and symposia at a fee, charging an access fee for non-members of the institutional community, marketing the library and its resources to the communities and churches in the neighborhood as well as within the college to increase usage. Librarians can also learn to write proposals for external funding of specific projects and not merely wait for the mother institutions.

## Staffing

As noted earlier, inadequate staffing is one of the perennial challenges facing theological libraries in Africa. In addition to staffing challenges, there is a shortage of opportunities for training in theological librarianship on the continent. Nonetheless, opportunities do exist. Most countries have library schools in one or more of their universities and tertiary institutions, offering training at the certificate, diploma, bachelor's, master's, and doctoral levels. Leading countries include South Africa, Nigeria, and Kenya, with each having more than fifteen library schools. Library staff is forced by circumstances to learn on the job to become theological librarians. This, however, is still a challenge since there is a lack of properly documented information resources on theological librarianship, and even what is available is not accessible to the librarians who need it. Many libraries have to do with student librarians on work-study or similar arrangements to address the inadequacy in staffing. However, there is a general concern that many theology students in Africa tend to be older and so struggle with trends in technology that they are not conversant with.

Training in theological librarianship needs to be emphasized from the top leadership of theological institutions and heads of theology departments. Librarians interested could be trained on an organized curriculum in theological librarianship, and especially in African theology.

## Information Resources

W. P. Wahl (2013) observes that the lack of necessary resources to provide good training in African theological schools impedes the advancement of theological education. Good resources create an enabling environment for training and so affect its quality. Most libraries struggle to find resources published in Africa or about African theology. Christoph Stückelberger (2013) lamented over the "limited theological production from the Global South, except in disciplines such as ecumenism, missiology, and contextual theologies." Having scanned through several catalogues of African theological colleges, seminaries, and universities, one notices that they are stocked with books written for Western education systems. This is because most of them were acquired as gifts and donations, with the librarians and the institutions having no say in their acquisition.

In departments of theology in academic libraries, the collection for theology is usually small and grows more slowly, especially because it is managed by general librarians just like any other discipline in the university. This varies with the size of the mother institution and the size of the theology department, which ultimately determines the size of the library collection on theology. Many African scholars need to be encouraged to publish local content that is relevant to the African context. There are initiatives like the Langham Partnership that seeks to develop biblical resources by local authors that are relevant to their contexts by sponsoring authors to write in their local contexts.

Access to the internet is increasing in most libraries on the continent and this brings the opportunities available on the internet for access to free digital resources closer. To supplement print copies, libraries would be better placed if the librarians, with the assistance of the faculty, developed a pool of digital resources relevant to their specific colleges and curricula.

Collaborations and networking are some of the initiatives that would greatly increase access to resources. This includes interlibrary cooperation that would provide resources from one library to users of another that may not have the information they need, as well as professional networking, cooperative purchasing, and shared subscription to e-resources. Existing Christian associations can play a bigger part in enhancing collaborations among theological librarians. Taking the case of Liberia, which has very limited opportunities for training in library science, whether short-term or long-term, collaborations with other parts of Africa that are well developed in librarianship could offer those opportunities. This applies to many other African countries that do not have library science training schools. Collaboration could lead to an establishment of a continental association of theological librarians that would give opportunities to the less privileged countries and help in developing theological librarianship on the continent.

There is a general feeling that the time for publicizing and developing theological librarianship is now and all efforts need to be put into making this a reality. However, there is a bigger challenge arising from the fact that theology is not a supported area of study in Africa. In Kenya, for example, the government offers scholarships for free tuition to students in universities who score a given grade but excludes those taking theology. Consequently, theological colleges have transformed into universities and now offer "popular" professional degree courses that attract both the students and government sponsorship. The effect of this move is that focus on collection development is leaning towards other courses, leaving theology behind.

## Conclusion

The concept of theological librarianship is not yet well understood in Africa and needs more engagement at all levels. Perhaps a curriculum and structured training will need to be developed for theological librarians. The development of theological libraries and librarianship in Africa is a call for concerted efforts. It requires deliberate and focused support from the administration of theological institutions and heads of departments of theology to succeed. Theological library associations and organizations at national and international levels have played a key role in developing libraries to where they are and will continue to play a leading role in the future. The rapid growth of Christianity on the continent requires that theological training is made solid and one way is by ensuring a strong base of resources to support the training of Christian workers and ministers. This gives theological libraries relevance in the growth of Christianity on the continent.

The exponential growth of internet usage on the continent provides an opportunity for maximizing the advantages of the internet in the provision of library services. Theological librarians need to be positioned to plug into technological developments on the continent by ensuring full automation of their processes and services. The increased ICT infrastructural development on the continent gives hope of increased access to theological resources.

Cooperation and collaboration are the way to go to realize economies of scale in the acquisition of resources and services for theological libraries. Therefore, theological librarians must go out of their way to collaborate if they are to meet the increasingly changing user needs. There is a need for a continental theological library association to enhance a concerted move to develop theological librarianship on the continent. This will give exposure and support of various kinds, especially to struggling libraries, and offer a forum for the exchange of information and skills among theological librarians.

## Notes

1. The Association for Christian Theological Education in Africa was formerly Accrediting Council for Theological Education in Africa and majorly dealt with accrediting theological schools the continent.

## Works Cited

Akporhonor, Blessings Amina. "Library Funding in Nigeria: Past, Present and Future." *The Bottom Line* 18, no. 2: 63–70. *https://doi.org/10.1108 /08880450510597505*.

Bailey-Hainer, Brenda. 2014. "Infinite Possibilities: The Future of Theological Librarianship." *The ANZTLA EJournal* 13. Accessed April 2, 2019. *http:// ejournal.anztla.org/anztla/article/viewFile/122/113*.

Bowers, Paul. 1989. "New Light on Theological Education in Africa." *ACTEA Tools and Studies* 9: 13–26. *http://www.acteaweb.org/downloads/tools/Tools%20and %20Studies%2009.pdf*.

Miniwatts Marketing Group. 2019. "Internet Users Statistics for Africa." Accessed April 2, 2019. *http://www.internetworldstats.com*.

Mudave, Ephraim. n.d. *Results of the Survey on the Status of Theological Libraries in Africa Conducted in February 2019*. Unpublished.

Neill, Stephen. 1964. *Christian Missions*. Harmondsworth, Middlesex: Penguin Books.

Stückelberger, Christoph. 2013. "Africa Goes Online: The Global Library for Theology and Ecumenism." In *Handbook of Theological Education in Africa*, edited by Dietrich Werner, 1093–1100. Oxford: Wipf and Stock Publishers.

Wahl, W.P. "Towards Relevant Theological Education in Africa: Comparing the International Discourse with Contextual Challenges." *Acta Theologica* 33, no. 1: 266–293. *http://dx.doi.org/10.4314/actat.v33i1.14*.

# CHAPTER 4

# Theological Libraries in Australia and New Zealand

KERRIE BURN

## Introduction

This chapter will outline the history and current state of theological librarianship in Australia and New Zealand.

The earliest theological libraries in both countries were often the private library collections of individual clerics. Over time, the development of theological libraries tended to be aligned with the development of theological teaching institutions. These were often denominationally-based and/or associated with seminaries or the formation houses of particular religious orders. The establishment of consortial arrangements between these theological teaching institutions has also been a feature of the theological education landscape. These have provided economies of scale, opportunities for collaboration, and access for members to an increased range of library resources. In the region, significant theological library collections are also located in the state and national libraries, and at some of the larger universities which have theology or religious studies departments. In addition to discussing the development of theological libraries, this chapter will include an overview of options for generalist librarianship education, outline the roles and status of the peak professional library associations in both countries (ALIA and LIANZA), and detail the professional development opportunities for those working in Australasian theological libraries. Integral to the work of theological libraries in this region is the Australian and New Zealand Theological Library Association (ANZTLA) and this chapter will elaborate on some of the historical achievements and current activities of the Association.

## Theological Libraries—History and Development

The development of theological libraries and theological education in Australia and New Zealand do not have identical histories but they do share many similarities. Theological libraries in both countries are generally associated with teaching institutions and/or affiliated with particular denominations, religious orders, or faith traditions. Several sources can provide further information about the institutional development of Australian theological education from its origins in the nineteenth century (Sherlock 2009, 21–38; Sherlock 2010; Ball 2018). The current theological education landscape is very different from what it was a century, or even a few decades, ago. In the colonial era, prior to the Federation of Australia in 1901, when the first universities were being established, theological education was regarded as inherently sectarian, potentially divisive, and was therefore treated with suspicion by the bodies governing higher education (Treloar 2009; Sherlock 2016). In Australia, the teaching of theology was often specifically prohibited by the charter of many older universities.[1] Theological education became the domain of particular religious denominations, for the members of each, in order to train for ministry or priesthood. This resulted in the earliest significant theological collections being developed by libraries associated with seminaries or theological teaching institutions rather than the larger universities. In Australia, the oldest pre-World War I universities, plus one or two elite universities established in the 1960s, form a network commonly named the 'sandstone universities,' which have eminence in Australia comparable to the Ivy Leagues in the United States or Oxford and Cambridge in the United Kingdom. Because the theological teaching institutions have not been seen as part of this older, established sandstone university environment, many theological institutions have spent a long time seeking recognition, establishing their consortia and eventually universities, and having their theological qualifications recognised by state and federal accreditation agencies.

Partly because of the decline in the number of individuals pursuing religious vocations in recent decades, and partly in pursuit of economies of scale and optimal use of scarce resources, many seminaries and/or religious orders have grouped to offer theological education and formation. Two examples are Catholic Theological College[2] and Yarra Theological Union,[3] both located in Melbourne. Similarly, teaching institutions have also grouped under the auspices of ecumenical degree-granting bodies, such as the University of Divinity,[4] the

Image 1: Mannix Library, Catholic Theological College, University of Divinity, Melbourne, Australia. © Mannix Library

Australian College of Theology,[5] and the Sydney College of Divinity.[6] Other similarly named consortia of theological schools in Australia have also been established in Adelaide,[7] Perth,[8] and Brisbane,[9] as well as in Auckland,[10] New Zealand. Such consortial arrangements have often been inspired by a spirit of ecumenism.[11] These partnerships have provided members with enhanced collaborative and resource-sharing opportunities and staff and students with access to a wider range of library resources.

In an age where Christian church attendance is on the decline, more students than ever are now engaging in some form of theological education. However, theological students are no longer destined only for clerical ministry within a particular denomination. Theological courses now have large numbers of lay students in addition to those studying as part of their pathway to ordained ministry or religious life. Many of these students will not identify as belonging to any specific denomination or faith tradition and may be studying with no particular vocational outcome in mind. There are now also a much wider variety of study programs available, including certificate and diploma courses, as well as bachelor's, master's, and doctoral degrees, with an ever-growing emphasis on research as well as teaching.

Moving against their earlier determinedly secular and anti-sectarian positions, Australian universities have more recently permitted the discipline of theology to be introduced either by institutional affiliation or even by internal inclusion as institutional departments or schools. This has altered the tertiary theological education landscape once again. Several theological colleges are now also affiliated with larger universities. For example, the Adelaide College of Divinity is affiliated with the Flinders University Department of Theology in South Australia. Government mechanisms of accreditation and registration have required many smaller institutions to enhance their quality to come up to higher education standards. Compliance requirements have also necessitated greater resourcing, which churches have generally been unable or unwilling to provide as independent institutions. Accordingly, they have either unified, joined consortia, or affiliated with universities. In the 1980s, state funding for approved theological education courses became available. This was a welcome development for many, and eligible students can now obtain low-interest government loans to cover the cost of their tuition. Theological teaching institutions in Australia and New Zealand tend to have modest endowments and those with limited additional sources of income risk becoming dependent on government sources of income. The need to comply with the requirements of the secular university system has created tensions within some theological institutions. The discipline of theology is now being taught alongside many other disciplines and is being assessed according to new criteria. This has required a reassessment of some long-held educational assumptions of the discipline that have carried over from a time when theology was being taught in a narrower context.

Institutional allegiances and membership of degree-granting consortia have not remained constant and over time some institutions have moved from one umbrella organisation to another. For example, three colleges that were formerly under the umbrella of the Brisbane College of Divinity are now associated with three different institutions: St Francis Theological College now offers its programs as part of Charles Sturt University, Trinity Theological College now offers its programs through the Adelaide College of Divinity, and St Paul's Theological College offers its programs through the Australian Catholic University. Accordingly, significant theological library collections in Australia and New Zealand are now associated with theology or religious studies departments at larger mainstream universities. Examples include the Australian Catholic University, Charles Sturt University, Notre Dame University, Flinders University, and Murdoch University in Australia, and the University of Auckland and the University of Otago in New Zealand.[12] State and national libraries in both countries also have significant theological collections. Theological librarians in Australia and New Zealand are therefore employed in a variety of institutions and

Image 2: National Library of Australia in Canberra. © National Library of Australia

are custodians of collections that range from smaller seminary or denomination-based libraries through to large multi-campus university, state, and national libraries.

Theological libraries themselves have also changed significantly over the years. Initially, aspiring ministers would have relied on more experienced ministers taking up the challenge of providing theological training, and students would have relied on access to the personal libraries of these more senior ministers. However, as both student numbers and resources grew, the need for better organisation, dedicated teaching staff, and professional librarians also grew. In today's world, where technology is integral to the provision of information and resources, a technologically well-equipped library is a must, as are appropriately qualified librarians with the expertise to manage this technology as well as traditional library services. Institutions offering theological education are continually seeking more effective approaches to the delivery of high-quality programs that will attract and engage new cohorts of students. The requirement to support research as well as teaching and learning in this rapidly changing environment has only increased the need for theological education providers to hire professional theological librarians with relevant expertise.

Ecumenical cooperation across teaching institutions has been a common feature of the theological education landscape in the region. This, in turn, has led to the associated libraries also undertaking ecumenical relationships. Historically, in Australia and New Zealand, theology has been studied in many small institutions separated by distance, denomination, and divisions within churches. Theological librarians often work in relatively isolated environments, either as solo librarians or because colleagues in similar institutions are located some distance away. Because each library must provide the basic tools for theological study there is a great deal of duplication and therefore less money for other resources. Cooperation forged through ecumenical partnerships has had considerable benefits for theological libraries in Australia and New Zealand. The benefits of collaboration have included the sharing of resources, the establishment of the Australian and New Zealand Theological Library Association, and the development of shared standards and other publications to assist all members of the Association. Several publications have arisen from collaborative library projects associated with the formerly mentioned ecumenical degree-granting bodies. These projects have mostly related to shared collection development, for example, a collaborative report about the resources of the Melbourne College of Divinity (now University of Divinity; Burn, Connelly, Roche, and Foster 1992) and a similar publication for the Sydney College of Divinity (Sydney College of Divinity 1992).

## Education for Theological Librarians

In Australia and New Zealand, there are no educational programs specifically designed for those wishing to work in theological libraries. Pathways to theological librarianship tend to involve the completion of a generalist professional library qualification coupled with an interest in working in the sector and subsequent experience and related professional development. In Australia, the peak professional library association, the Australian Library & Information Association (ALIA), accredits all courses in library and information management, including diploma, bachelor's, graduate diploma, and master's programs. The Library and Information Association of New Zealand Aotearoa (LIANZA) is New Zealand's equivalent to ALIA and performs a similar accreditation role. This accreditation role ensures the quality of courses and their relevance to the current and emerging library and information practice. In both countries, library and information science education has undergraduate as well as postgraduate pathways that provide eligibility for membership of the national professional library associations.

The employment outcomes differ depending on the course undertaken and the qualification level obtained. In Australia, professional librarians and information specialists complete undergraduate and postgraduate university courses. Those wishing to work as library technicians complete diploma-level courses that generally lead to paraprofessional positions. Additionally, there are some courses specifically designed for teacher-librarians. These are postgraduate university courses where prospective students must already be teacher-qualified to be eligible to enroll. No formal qualification is required for library assistant roles, however many Technical and Further Education (TAFE) Colleges and private vocational education providers offer Certificate II, III, and IV in library and information services. Although not required, the completion of these certificate level courses may improve an applicant's employment prospects for library assistant positions. Most job advertisements for librarians and information specialists or teacher-librarians include selection criteria stating that applicants must be eligible for ALIA Associate Membership (AALIA), while library technician roles will stipulate eligibility for ALIA Library Technician Membership (ALIATec). ALIA is also the body that determines whether professional library qualifications obtained overseas are recognised.

The basis for all ALIA-accredited courses is meeting a set of standards developed by educators, practitioners, and employers from the industry. These are detailed in *The Library and Information Sector: Core Knowledge, Skills and Attributes* (ALIA 2014) and the *Foundation Knowledge, Skills and Attributes Relevant to Information Professionals Working in Archives, Libraries and Records Management* (ALIA 2015). There are a variety of study options and course names vary widely depending on the institution and the emphasis given to different components of the curriculum. However, all graduates of the courses below would be eligible to become ALIA Associate Members (AALIA). Those undertaking a graduate diploma or master's degree would generally already have completed a minimum 3-year bachelor's degree.

In contrast, courses in Australia that provide eligibility for ALIA Library Technician Membership (ALIATec) have the same award name, i.e. the Diploma of Library and Information Services. Approximately fifteen institutions across Australia currently offer this award. ALIA also accredits the Diploma of Library and Information Services award offered in Fiji at Pacific Technical and Further Education (Pacific TAFE), The University of the South Pacific. The first class of this Fiji award graduated on 21 March 2019 (ALIA 2019). All courses accredited by ALIA, leading to both professional librarian and library technician qualifications and awards, are offered in a variety of study modes including on-campus, online, and blended options.

| Charles Sturt University | Bachelor of Information Studies (with specialisations) Master of Information Studies (with specialisations) |
|---|---|
| Curtin University, Perth, Western Australia | Bachelor of Arts (Librarianship and Corporate Information Management) Graduate Diploma in Information and Library Studies Master of Information Management |
| Monash University, Melbourne, Victoria | Master of Business Information Systems |
| Open Universities Australia | Bachelor of Arts (Librarianship and Corporate Information Management) Graduate Diploma in Information and Library Studies Master of Information Management |
| RMIT University, Melbourne, Victoria | Master of Information Management |
| University of South Australia | Graduate Diploma in Information and Library Studies Master of Information Management |
| University of Technology Sydney, New South Wales | Graduate Diploma in Digital Information Management Master of Digital Information Management |

*Table 1: Bachelor's and graduate courses in LIS in Australia.*

In New Zealand, two tertiary institutions offer professional-level library qualifications. These include:

- Master of Information Studies (MIS) with the Libraries Specialisation (LIBS)–Victoria University of Wellington
- Bachelor of Applied Science with Information and Library Studies (ILS) major–Open Polytechnic of New Zealand
- Bachelor of Arts with ILS major or double major with ILS / Humanities or ILS / Communication–Open Polytechnic of New Zealand
- Bachelor of Library and Information Studies–Open Polytechnic of New Zealand

In addition to these bachelor's degrees and master's awards, Victoria University of Wellington and Open Polytechnic of New Zealand also offer other awards, including a range of diplomas and certificates as well as a PhD programme. There are also diploma and certificate awards offered by Te Wananga-o-Raukawa. This institution's courses develop bilingual and bicultural managers of Māori information resources in Māori and non-Māori organisations.

## Professional Development

ALIA is also involved in supporting the professional development (PD) of those working in the sector. Graduates of ALIA-accredited courses are eligible to commence their certified professional membership after joining the ALIA PD Scheme. The scheme has been operating since 2000 and enables members to accumulate points for various activities. The scheme provides a framework whereby participants can demonstrate their commitment to ongoing learning and achieve formal recognition in the process. The huge range of eligible activities means that it is relatively easy to accumulate the required points. Certificates are awarded after accumulating points for several years and participants are able to add an extra post-nominal, AALIA (CP) or AFALIA (CP) or ALIATec (CP), to their name. ALIA has also introduced a number of subject specialisations as an extension to its PD Scheme. These specialisations allow members to focus their learning on subject-related competencies. While there is no specific subject specialisation for those staff working in theological libraries, it will generally be the case that the competencies associated with ALIA's Research/Academic Specialisation are of relevance to those working in theological libraries, and activities for this area of specialisation will also be of interest to theological librarians. Another ALIA PD Scheme of interest may be the Heritage Collections Specialisation which was launched on 1 July 2019. It is designed for ALIA members interested in special collections, rare books, and the preservation of heritage materials. Members of ALIA's PD scheme will also receive a weekly email that includes information about a range of training and professional development opportunities (including a number of free activities). Because librarians need to continually engage with new technologies and changes in the higher education environment, a commitment to lifelong learning beyond an initial qualification is essential to remain current in the profession.

The New Zealand library association has taken a slightly different approach to supporting professional development by introducing a Professional Registration Scheme. LIANZA's website states that:

> The Professional Registration scheme was introduced by LIANZA in 2007, in order to increase the standing of the Library and Information profession in New Zealand, recognise professional excellence and continuing professional development, and provide a mechanism by which employers can coach and develop their professional staff. The scheme also provides an assurance for future employers, both in New Zealand and overseas, that the registrant meets professional standards of competency in the body of knowledge and ethics required for library and information work.

Once registered, members are able to use the 'RLIANZA' post-nominal and also become an Associate of LIANZA. It is worth noting that one of the eligibility criteria for becoming professionally registered is being an individual member of a professional library and information management association, and the Australian and New Zealand Theological Library Association (ANZTLA) is listed as one of these recognised associations. An annual registration fee is charged and paid with LIANZA membership, and every three years members of the scheme must demonstrate that they have been actively participating in PD activities by completing and submitting a journal to the Professional Registration Board.

Unfortunately, not all theological librarians in Australia and New Zealand are members of ALIA or LIANZA and so they are not able to take advantage of the opportunities that the national professional associations provide. A survey of ANZTLA members in 2016 revealed that while 95% were eligible for ALIA membership, only 50% were actually members, and only 26% were also current members of ALIA's PD scheme (Burn 2019). In addition to being supported in their ongoing learning and professional development, members of the professional associations receive publications and e-newsletters to keep them abreast of industry news and developments in the library and information community. They also receive access to specialist eBooks and over 180 full-text journal titles via a library science database and a range of member discounts. While anyone can access the general information available via the ALIA and LIANZA websites, additional resources can only be accessed through the member portal, which requires a login. Beyond their membership of ANZTLA and the national library associations, there have always been a small number of libraries and individual librarians that have also engaged with theological library associations from beyond their own region, becoming members, attending conferences, and working on international collaborations.[13]

## The Australian and New Zealand Theological Library Association (ANZTLA)

In Australia and New Zealand, those working in theological libraries are more likely to maintain professional networks with members of ANZTLA, with PD opportunities also achieved via the Association. Historically, ANZTLA has played a vital role in the development and ongoing work of theological libraries in the region. This region is sometimes more broadly defined as "Australasia," which includes some neighbouring islands in the South Pacific as well as Australia and New Zealand. ANZTLA's mission states that it "seeks to foster the study of theology and religion by enhancing the development of theological and religious libraries and librarianship." While the unofficial beginnings of ANZTLA may date from as early as 1977, officially it came into being in 1985. It developed initially as a consequence of a series of library consultations of the Australian & New Zealand Association of Theological Schools (ANZATS) held in 1978, 1979, 1983, 1984 and 1985. The history of the development of ANZTLA has been documented in more detail elsewhere (Zweck 1986 and 1996; Robinson 2010), including the early decision to form an association of theological librarians that was separate from ANZATS (Zweck 1985). Although ANZTLA membership initially included the 57 libraries of ANZATS schools, it was also open to the involvement of other libraries or individuals with interests in the fields of theology or religious studies. The Association's constitution was initially drafted in 1986 and, after further revisions, adopted in August 1987. ANZTLA subsequently decided to incorporate at its Annual General Meeting in 2001. The ANZTLA website's membership pages now act as a directory of theological libraries in Australia and New Zealand as well as providing membership information. The original data in the current online membership directory was based on a 2006 print version. The online version enables member libraries to update their own records. Ideally, this would ensure that information was always current, but this is contingent on all members being vigilant about maintaining up-to-date data for their own institutions. At the time of writing, ANZTLA membership included approximately eighty institutions (with about five having two to three libraries), eight individual members and twelve life members.

## ANZTLA Activities

ANZTLA holds an annual conference and maintains an email discussion list. These communication modes are important as theological librarians in Australia and New Zealand are often working part-time or solo, with limited time or funds to be involved with their national professional library associations. The conference and email forum also help to promote inter-library co-operation. Other activities of the Association include maintaining a website, coordinating several consortia for the purchase of online databases, and publishing literature and information related to theological librarianship, including ANZTLA Standards and the *ANZTLA eJournal*. Further information about some of these activities is detailed below.

## Conferences

The annual ANZTLA conference has been held every year since the inaugural conference was held in Canberra in 1986, when it was attended by twenty-six librarians. This is a remarkable achievement given the vast distances involved and the relatively small membership of the Association. Theological libraries in

Image 3: Attendees of the 2018 ANZTLA conference. ©ANZTLA

Australia and New Zealand are often separated by significant geographical distances. The conference location now rotates each year through the cities of Melbourne, Auckland (or another city in New Zealand), Canberra, Perth, Brisbane, Sydney, and Adelaide, with members from the ANZTLA chapter in each region being responsible for organising the conference. Conferences provide an opportunity for members to come together, network, catch up on trends in librarianship, share their experiences, be informed and inspired by a range of presentations, and visit locations of professional interest in the host city. For many years ANZTLA has also used scholarship funds to sponsor individuals from theological libraries in the South Pacific to attend the annual conference. This sponsorship can also be an opportunity for recipients to network, visit Australian and New Zealand theological libraries in the host city, and develop partnerships with colleagues from other countries.

In addition to the annual ANZTLA Conference, there are also some regional networks that meet as chapters several times per year, generally in cities where there is a significant concentration of local ANZTLA members within easy mutual traveling distance. These regional networks provide additional opportunities for face-to-face meetings, sharing of experiences, interim updating on projects, and working together.

## ANZTLA-Forum

The ANZTLA-forum is an email discussion list for ANZTLA members and others interested in theological librarianship in Australia, New Zealand, and the Pacific. This online forum was established in 1988 and is an extension of the in-person relationships forged through connections at conferences and regional chapter meetings. The collegiality evident on the forum is certainly a strength of the organisation. The ANZTLA-forum facilitates communication between members, allowing them to share news, ask questions, and respond to issues under discussion. It is also a place where those new to theological librarianship can raise issues and have them addressed in a supportive environment.

## ANZTLA Collaborative Projects

Collaboration has always been a hallmark of ANZTLA, and this focus has enabled many cooperative projects to advance despite the differing denominational affiliations and religious beliefs (or lack of religious beliefs) of individual members. Over the years, ANZTLA members have contributed to numerous projects with outcomes intended to be of benefit to all members of the association. ANZTLA has produced several significant publications throughout its history that have proved to be invaluable resources for theological librarians, academic staff, students, and researchers.

### i. Australasian Religion Index (ARI)

*ARI* (*http://app.anztla.org/AriAbout.aspx*) is an author, subject, and scriptural passage index covering over eighty religious and theological serials published in Australia and New Zealand. A print version of *ARI* was published annually from 1989 to 2008, after which the *ARI* database became available online. This online version contains the full contents of *ARI* from v. 1 (1989) to the present. The future of *ARI* was recently reviewed by ANZTLA. Issues considered included the ongoing difficulty in sourcing enough indexers from within the ANZTLA membership, the fact that much of *ARI*'s content was now indexed in other databases, and the increased availability of these databases at ANZTLA-member institutions. At a meeting held at the ANZTLA conference in July 2019 the decision was made to cease publication of *ARI*.

### ii. Australasian Union List of Serials in Theological Collections (AULOTS)

*AULOTS* (*http://app.anztla.org/AulotsAbout.aspx*) is another ANZTLA publication. Several editions were published in print format (with different editors), the latest being the fourth edition, which was compiled and edited by Tony McCumstie and published in 2002. The data from this final print version was used to produce the current online version. *AULOTS* currently contains holdings information for approximately 5,200 print theological and religious serials held in approximately 100 libraries in Australia and New Zealand. The online database can be searched by serial title and provides links to library holdings statements and library contact details. Historically, *AULOTS* has been a vital resource for libraries and institutions, fostering inter-library cooperation at both regional and national levels, and useful for facilitating interlibrary loan traffic and for identifying journal titles and extent of holdings in other library collections. The earlier print version was a vital research tool in a time where most Australasian libraries were not automated and had no access to national databases. The accuracy of the online version relies on members updating their own serial holdings data. However, as more and more theological libraries become members of Libraries Australia or *Te Puna Search* (New Zealand's national library database – https://tepuna.on.worldcat.org/discovery) and can access holdings data via Australia's Trove (https://trove.nla.gov.au/) or WorldCat, *AULOTS* may also eventually face a future review by ANZTLA.

### iii. ANZTLA EJournal

The *ANZTLA EJournal* is the official publication of the Australian and New Zealand Theological Library Association. Formerly the *ANZTLA Newsletter* (1987–2007), the title continues to be published twice per year. It contains news, articles, book reviews, library profiles, papers delivered at the Association's annual conference, reports, and other items, all directed to an audience comprising anyone interested in theological librarianship. Content primarily covers theological librarianship in the Australasian region, but many articles will also be of interest and relevance to a wider, international audience. The title became the *ANZTLA EJournal* from 2008 and it is now open access and hosted by Atla using the Open Journal Systems software.

### iv. ANZTLA Statistics

For each year since 1984, statistics have been compiled from data that has been provided by ANZTLA member libraries on a voluntary basis. This collated data provides an overview of library information related to institution type and population, denominational affiliation, staffing levels, patron types and loan periods, collection resources (including monograph, serials, and databases), library facilities, library expenditure and management, and classification system information. This rich data often proves useful when an individual library is advocating for an increase in budget or staffing levels at their institution. It provides a capability to compare statistics with similarly-sized libraries or those from an equivalent context. It remains a constant challenge to get all libraries to complete the annual statistical questionnaire, and the resulting gaps in the data can be a limitation to the value of the overall exercise. A summary of the data is compiled each year by the ANZTLA statistician and published in the *ANZTLA EJournal*.

### v. ANZTLA Standards

One of the goals itemised in ANZTLA's mission is to "educate persons on acceptable standards of librarianship among theological and religious libraries, and to support the implementation and development of such standards." The first standards document was formally adopted by ANZTLA on 9 September 1988 and subsequently received endorsement by the Australian Library and Information Association in 1989 and the New Zealand Library Association in 1991. The ANZTLA standards are designed to assist theological institutions, librarians, faculty members, library users, and members of accrediting bodies and other interested persons in the provision and evaluation of library services, resources, and facilities. The ANZTLA website notes that:

> *Theological institutions in Australasia, and hence their libraries, vary markedly with respect to their functions, the levels of courses offered, the nature and size of their faculties and student bodies. For these reasons the standards do not reflect a quantitative approach for measuring the adequacy of library budgets, staffing, collections or spaces. Rather, in synthesising professional experience and expectations, they reflect a qualitative approach.*

The ANZTLA standards were last ratified at the Association's Annual General Meeting in July 2000. They could, therefore, benefit from review and updating to ensure their ongoing relevance and currency.

### vi. Consortia

One of the additional member benefits of ANZTLA institutional membership is the availability of ANZTLA consortium rates for a number of databases. These offerings include *Atla Religion Database, AtlaSerials, AtlaSerials PLUS, Old Testament Abstracts, New Testament Abstracts, EBSCO Religion & Philosophy Collection, ProQuest Religion Database,* and *Oxford Biblical Studies Online.* There are also ANZTLA subscription discounts on select Sage journal titles and several Brill databases.

## ANZTLA Member Contributions

Some theological librarians in Australia and New Zealand see their work as a vocation. Others are professional librarians first and theology is the subject area in which they develop expertise, in a similar way to those working in other subject-based academic libraries. Irrespective of their motivation, throughout its history ANZTLA has been shaped by members who have made significant contributions to the understanding and development of theological libraries and librarianship. Some of these contributions have resulted in publications. Others have presented at conferences or participated in collaborative projects that have benefited the wider theological community, such as the development of the website and other key resources and the establishment of consortia. ANZTLA has developed several ways of honouring these individuals.

The Jeannette Little Sponsorship Scheme is administered by ANZTLA and was established to honour Jeannette's memory and her many years of dedicated service to theological libraries and librarians in the South Pacific region. The librarian at Pacific Theological College in Suva, Fiji for approximately 10 years (1990–2000) and then at Trinity Theological College in Brisbane (2001–2003), Jeannette travelled widely in the Pacific region, worked as the Library Consultant to the South Pacific Association of Theological Schools (SPATS), and was responsible for organising basic training programmes for librarians working in small theological libraries in the South Pacific. The Sponsorship Scheme contributes to the PD of theological librarians from islands in the South Pacific. Grants can provide funding for further study or training, attendance at conferences, purchase of professional resources, and other activities. Libraries in the region may also be provided with free ANZTLA membership and access to the *Australasian Religion Index Online*. Recipients who attend the ANZTLA conference are expected to make a short presentation about their library at the conference and prepare a written report for the ANZTLA Board which may subsequently be published in the *ANZTLA EJournal*.

Trevor Zweck was a former librarian at the Australian Lutheran College Library in South Australia. After being involved with the earlier ANZATS library consultations, he became ANZTLA's founding president in 1985 and continued to hold this position until his premature death in 1996. Zweck was proactive, practical, and visionary, seeing the value of cooperation among theological libraries in Australasia and encouraging all libraries to contribute to these beneficial collaborations. Zweck was a dedicated advocate for theological libraries, worked on the development of standards for libraries of the ANZATS, and authored several articles on the subject, even prior to ANZTLA being officially established. He continued to present at conferences and contribute articles and book reviews to many journals. His significant contributions to the theological library sector were acknowledged by ANZTLA when it instituted the Trevor Zweck Award in his honour, an award that recognises individuals who have also made significant contributions to the development of theological libraries and librarianship in the region.

One example, Hans Arns, played a key role in the initial development of the *Australasian Union List of Serials in Theological Collections*, which was first published in 1983. In 2014 Hans Arns received the *Trevor Zweck Award* to recognise his work on the "Sharing the World ELibrary" project (*http:// sharingtheword.info*). This online resource was created to provide access to a comprehensive collection of open access materials (including books, journal articles, periodical titles, theses, church documents, audio/visual resources, and podcasts), initially for use in Catholic seminaries in countries which lack access to adequate theological libraries but now available to all.

Other publications of note by ANZTLA members include Lawrence D. McIntosh's *A Style Manual for the Presentation of Papers and Theses in Religion and Theology*, published in 1994, and *So Great a Cloud of Witnesses: Libraries & Theologies*, edited by Philip Harvey and Lynn Pryor. This latter book was published in print in 1995 but is now available open access at *https://books.atla .com/index.php/atlapress/catalog/book/10*.


## Challenges and Opportunities

Many of the issues that theological librarians face today are the same as the ones that they have faced in the past, including collection development on a limited budget, limited professional development opportunities, and a general lack of recognition of their professional qualifications and expertise. Operating in the digital age has its own issues, such as the challenge of addressing the digital divide, providing access to the most relevant resources in a blended learning and resource environment, and constantly responding to change as new technologies emerge. Within the ecumenical consortia of multiple teaching institutions, tensions may also exist between collaborative versus competitive priorities.

Librarians often seem to fall in the "blind spot" for academics and theological educators rather than being identified and valued for the significant role they play as part of the theological education team. Assessment of libraries is part of standard national accreditation processes for higher education institutions, and having sufficient library resources is essential to the achievement of excellence in theological education. However, despite their professional qualifications and the integral role they play, the status of theological librarians is often overlooked and their contributions not valued or recognised. For example, in a recent publication about the development, challenges, and future of theological education in Australia (Bain, Hussey, and Sutherland 2018), no author in any of its twenty-one chapters discusses the place of libraries or librarians. Several authors note recent pedagogical innovations in theological education, facilitated by rapid advances in digital technology and the increased use of digital platforms and web-based communication systems. However, there is no corresponding acknowledgment of the dramatic transition from print to e-resources and the resulting managerial complexities faced by librarians. There still seems to be a view of librarians as 'service providers' rather than professionals in their own right. Although there will be some exceptions to this trend, there is clearly still a lot more to be done to highlight the role of the library and librarians in the theological education process in this region of the world.

As well as having a subordinate or peripheral status within their theological education institutions, theological librarians may also be a blind spot within the wider library and information profession. In a book published in 2009 about international librarianship (Abdullahi), there were several contributions in the section related to library development in Australia and New Zealand. In the chapter on academic libraries, no higher education institutions teaching theology were mentioned. In the chapter dealing with special libraries, while theology/religious libraries are included as a category of a special library, no further information is provided, despite ANZTLA having existed since 1985. Other types of special libraries are elaborated on, as are a number of their related special interest groups or professional associations. This absence aligns with an earlier observation of mine that:

> *Although theological library networks are very active within Australia and New Zealand, these networks do not tend to be very well known within the Australian Library and Information Association (ALIA) or the wider Australian library community in the same way as other existing special library networks such as Law or Health libraries (Burn 2007, 1).*

With fewer individuals identifying as Christian and declining church attendance in Australasia, the unfortunate result is that there are fewer individuals with a background in theology applying for roles in theological libraries. This can make appointing new librarians in theological libraries very difficult. Employing institutions will often be in the position of needing to employ a professionally trained librarian who has little or no theological background. There is often then a preference for employing individuals with a background in the humanities. This situation led librarians at the University of Divinity to successfully propose in 2019 that newly appointed librarians with limited or no theological background be able to undertake theological studies at the appointing institution as part of their employment contract. While some theological librarians have generalist roles, others working at larger institutions may have more specialist roles. Those seeking such roles may be expected to have already theological studies in addition to having expertise in areas such as information technology, data management, education, special collections, or conservation studies.

## Conclusion

The history and development of theological libraries in Australia and New Zealand can be seen as a parallel story to that of the theological education institutions with which they are associated. Libraries and librarians from this region will also share similar experiences and challenges to those from other parts of the world. There will also be aspects that are unique to Australia and New Zealand because of a range of historical, geographic, and other factors. Throughout their shared history, theological librarians in Australia and New Zealand have overcome many challenges by working together and have achieved much in this process. The contributions of many individuals over many years have resulted in the publication of new resources and other achievements of benefit to local theological librarians as well as those further afield. Integral to the work of theological libraries in the region has been the Australian and New Zealand Theological Library Association (ANZTLA), and the Association has been responsible for shaping the education and professional development of many members. Theological librarians have long recognised the benefits of taking a collective approach. Library cooperation has been a hallmark of much that ANZTLA has achieved and theological libraries in Australia and New Zealand, as well as in the rest of the world, are all the richer for it.

## Notes

1. The first Australian universities, e.g. the University of Sydney (founded 1850) and the University of Melbourne (founded 1853) intentionally excluded the teaching of theology. Major denominations participated in theological education through residential colleges that were established by churches on university land. See Harding 2018; Piggin 1997; Banks 1976 and 1977.
2. Catholic Theological College (CTC) was established in 1972 by a group of dioceses and religious orders that agreed to act together as a confederated body in academic matters. This federation currently comprises the Archdioceses of Melbourne and Hobart, the Dioceses of Ballarat, Sandhurst, and Sale, the Oblates of Mary Immaculate, the Salesians of Don Bosco, the Conventual Franciscan Friars, the Dominican Friars, the Missionaries of God's Love, the Society of Jesus (Jesuits), and the Society of the Divine Saviour (Salvatorians).

CTC also has seminarians attending from other dioceses and formation houses including the Archdiocese of Adelaide, the Diocese of Port Pirie, Darwin, Wollongong, and the Capuchin Friars.

3. Yarra Theological Union (YTU) was originally founded in 1971 by the Carmelites, the Franciscans, the Missionaries of the Sacred Heart, and the Passionists. Over the years, other Catholic religious orders joined: the Redemptorists (Australian and New Zealand Provinces), Pallottines, Dominicans, Divine Word Missionaries, the Discalced Carmelites, and the Blessed Sacrament Congregation.

4. The University of Divinity, formerly the Melbourne College of Divinity, was incorporated by an Act of the Parliament of Victoria in 1910. The University offers a range of awards from graduate diplomas through to doctoral degrees via both face-to-face and online units.

5. The Australian College of Theology exists as a partnership between sixteen colleges of the Anglican Church of Australia and a confessionally diverse, national network of Bible and theological colleges.

6. The Sydney College of Divinity is a consortium made up of eight member institutions, which are the owners of SCD. It began in 1983 as a consortium of theological colleges in Sydney but now provides theological education across Australia, in New Zealand, and by distance across the world.

7. The Adelaide Theological Library was formed in 1997 and supports the teaching and research of the Adelaide College of Divinity and the Flinders University Department of Theology.

8. The Perth College of Divinity (PCD) came into being in 1985. It was an initiative of the Western Australian chapter of the Australia and New Zealand Association of Theological Schools (ANZATS) and brought together under one umbrella organization a number of theological education institutions located in Perth, Western Australia. The PCD has an Affiliation Agreement with Murdoch University and, on the basis of this agreement, the University began offering degrees in theology from 1986, with teaching staff initially coming from PCD institutions.

9. The Brisbane College of Theology was an ecumenical theological education consortium, comprising three colleges, St Francis Theological College (Anglican), St Paul's Theological College (Roman Catholic) and Trinity Theological College (Uniting Church), that operated from 1983–2009.

10. The Auckland Consortium for Theological Education (ACTE) was constituted in 1985 with initial members including St John's Theological College, Trinity College, and the Baptist Theological College. The ACTE was an Associated Teaching Institute of the Melbourne College of Divinity (now University of Di-

vinity) for a short time but since 2002 the teaching of theology has been done under the auspices of the University of Auckland's School of Theology.

11. For example, the University of Divinity (formerly the Melbourne College of Divinity) was initially a consortium representing the Anglican, Baptist, Congregational, Methodist, and Presbyterian Churches. An amendment to the Act of the Parliament of Victoria on which it was founded in 1972 saw the subsequent admission of the Churches of Christ and the Catholic Church in Victoria. The University now has eleven associated colleges representing the Anglican, Baptist (2), Catholic (3), Churches of Christ, Lutheran, Salvation Army, Coptic Orthodox, and Uniting Churches in Australia. However, ecumenical harmony has not always been ubiquitous in this part of the world. Morling College, a Baptist theological college located in New South Wales, was one of the founding colleges of the Sydney College of Divinity (SCD) in 1983. In 1989 it withdrew from the SCD on the grounds that Catholics were involved. Morling College is now an affiliated institution with the Australian College of Theology and a College of the University of Divinity.

12. The University of Auckland was established in 1883 and is the largest university in New Zealand. The country has a total of eight universities, the oldest being the University of Otago (established in 1869), which commenced offering the Bachelor of Theology degree in 1972. Both Auckland and Otago universities offer a variety of undergraduate and postgraduate awards in theology and religious studies. University of Otago courses are offered through its Department of Theology and Religion. The Hewitson Library at the Knox Centre for Ministry and Leadership in Dunedin is available to University of Otago students in addition to the resources of the University's Central Library. As of the time of writing, the University of Auckland website notes that the Bachelor of Theology degree and the Graduate Diploma in Theology have been suspended with no further admissions into this programme from 2015. Undergraduate students now need to take a major in theological and religious studies as part of a Bachelor of Arts degree. Postgraduate students can enroll in a Master of Theology degree or undertake doctoral studies. Other theological education institutions in New Zealand that are Institutional members of ANZATS include Carey Baptist College, Good Shepherd College (member of the Sydney College of Divinity), Laidlaw College (a member of the Australian College of Theology), St John's Theological College, and Trinity Methodist Theological College.

13. International theological library associations include the Association of British Theological and Philosophical Libraries (ABTAPL), Atla (established in 1946 as the American Theological Library Association), Bibliothèques Eu-

ropéennes de Théologie (BETH), and the Forum of Asian Theological Librarians (ForATL).

## Works Cited

Abdullahi, Ismael, ed. 2009. *Global Library and Information Science: A Textbook for Students and Educators: With Contributions from Africa, Asia, Australia, New Zealand, Europe, Latin America and the Caribbean, the Middle East, and North America.* IFLA Publications. München: K. G. Saur. *https://doi.org/10.1515/9783598441349.*

ALIA. 2019. "First Graduates of ALIA Accredited Course in Fiji." *ALIA Weekly* 7, no. 12. *https://www.alia.org.au/news/18377/first-graduates-alia-accredited-course-fiji.*

———. 2015. "Foundation Knowledge, Skills and Attributes Relevant to Information Professionals Working in Archives, Libraries and Records Management." *https://www.alia.org.au/foundation-knowledge-skills-and-attributes-relevant-information-professionals-working-archives.*

———. 2014. "The Library and Information Sector: Core Knowledge, Skills and Attributes." *https://www.alia.org.au/about-alia/policies-standards-and-guidelines/library-and-information-sector-core-knowledge-skills-and-attributes.*

Bain, Andrew M., Ian Hussey, and Martin P. Sutherland, eds. 2018. *Theological Education: Foundations, Practices, and Future Directions.* Australian College of Theology Monograph Series. Eugene, OR: Wipf and Stock.

Ball, Les. 2018. "A Thematic History of Theological Education in Australia." In *Theological Education: Foundations, Practices, and Future Directions*, edited by Andrew M. Bain, Ian Hussey, and Martin P. Sutherland, 88–100. Australian College of Theology Monograph Series. Eugene, OR: Wipf and Stock.

Banks, Robert. 1977. "Fifty Years of Theology in Australia, 1915–1965." *Colloquium* 9, no. 2: 7–16.

———. 1976. "Fifty Years of Theology in Australia, 1915–1965." *Colloquium* 8, no. 1: 36–42.

Burn, Kerrie. 2019. "ANZTLA and the ALIA Professional Development Scheme: A Survey." *The ANZTLA EJournal* 22: 6–14.

———. 2007. "The Australian Baptist Heritage Collection: Management of a Geographically Distributed Special Collection." Master's thesis, Melbourne College of Divinity.

———, Stephen Connelly, Thea Roche, and Siobhan Foster. 2000. *Theological Library Resources in the Melbourne College of Divinity: A Collaborative Report.* Victoria, Australia: Australia and New Zealand Theological Libraries Association.

Harding, Mark. 2018. "The Current Environment of Theological Education in Australia." In *Theological Education: Foundations, Practices, and Future Directions*, edited by Andrew M. Bain, Ian Hussey, and Martin P. Sutherland, 274–86. Australian College of Theology Monograph Series. Eugene, OR: Wipf and Stock.

Piggin, Stuart. 1997. "A History of Theological Education in Australia." In *The Furtherance of Religious Beliefs: Essays on the History of Theological Education in Australia*, edited by Geoffrey R. Treloar, 24–43. Sydney: Centre for the Study of Australian Christianity for the Evangelical History Association of Australia.

Robinson, Kim. 2010. "ANZTLA Keynote Address: ANZTLA, 25 years: A Sterling Achievement." *The ANZTLA EJournal* 5: 25–33.

Sherlock, Charles. 2010. "Australian Theological Education: An Historical and Thematic Overview." In *Handbook of Theological Education in World Christianity*, edited by Dietrich Werner, David Esterline, Namsoon Kang, and Joshva Raja, 458–465. Dorpspruit, South Africa: Cluster.

———. 2009. *Uncovering Theology: The Depth, Reach and Utility of Australian Theological Education.* Adelaide: ATF.

Sherlock, Peter. 2016. "The Foundation of the Melbourne College of Divinity." *Journal of Religious History* 40, no. 2: 204–24.

Sydney College of Divinity. 1992. *Sydney College of Divinity: Joint Collection Development Policy for the Libraries of the Sydney College of Divinity, May 1992, with the Individual Collection Development Policies of the Libraries of Member Institutions of the S. C. D., and the S. C. D. Library Evaluation Project Report, August 1990.* Manly, NSW: Sydney College of Divinity.

Treloar, Geoffrey R. 2009. "Towards a Master Narrative: Theological Learning and Teaching in Australia since 1901." *St Mark's Review* 210: 31–51.

Zweck, Trevor John. "Australian and New Zealand Theological Libraries and Librarianship Today: The Impact of the Australian and New Zealand Theological Library Association in Its First Decade." *American Theological Library Association Summary of Proceedings* 50: 175–87.

———. 1986. "Australian and New Zealand Theological Libraries and Librarianship." *American Theological Library Association Summary of Proceedings* 40: 88–100.

———. 1985 (October). "Theological Library Association Formed." *Colloquium: the Australian and New Zealand Theological Review* 18, no. 1: 71.

# CHAPTER 5

# Theological Libraries in Central and Western Europe

MATINA ĆURIĆ

## Introduction

Theological and religious libraries have a long and rich history in Europe's collective memory and an important role in the preservation of the entire Western cultural history and heritage. For centuries these libraries were in the center of European thought and scientific research and were responsible for the creation of library infrastructure and public reading systems in many countries. Even today many of the most valuable European library collections and cultural heritage are in the possession of churches, mosques, synagogues, and other religion-related institutions and libraries.

This contribution aims to provide an overview of these libraries across Europe, particularly its Central and Western part, which covers today more than 30 countries and has about 500 million inhabitants. This is not an easy task, not only because of the number of countries to be considered and the diversity in cultures, languages, religions, policies, and socio-economic situations, but also because theological librarianship is very heterogenous and operates in a complex environment which varies from country to country, and is determined by socio-political and religious history, as well as changes in higher education. Another major challenge is the lack of comparative and cross-country research on European theological libraries. There is a fairly large amount of scholarly literature on the history of individual theological and religious libraries in European countries but very few contemporary and over-arching approaches and studies (Geuns and Wolf-Dahm 1998; Geuns 1999 and 2000; Penner 2005; Dupont and Langlois 2011) in the field.

The situation of theological libraries across Europe, as described here, is mainly based on existing literature and information that has been gathered from theological library associations, their representatives, and websites. The contribution is organized into six sections (Brief History and Development; Current Status; European Theological Education and Libraries; Library Education Programs; Theological Library Associations; Challenges and Opportunities) and is meant to at least partially cover the above information gap and provide general information for new and future librarians or anyone interested in the subject of European theological librarianship.

## Brief History and Development

Europe boasts a very rich history of libraries, in which theological and religious ones play a dominant role for almost 1,000 years (approximately from the 5th to the 15th century AD). In this chapter, only major types of theological libraries and development phases will be mentioned. For more information about general library history in the Western world (e.g. Harris 1999; Staikos 2004–2013; Battles 2015) and libraries in the specific period, references are provided.

In Europe, as in most parts of the world, the first known libraries originated in the proximity of temples. Temple collections were among the earliest forms of both the proto-library and theological library on the European continent. Although references to temple libraries in Ancient Greece can be found (Harris 1999, 50; Murphy 2013), these libraries were more common in the Roman empire. Apart from serving for the education and training of priests, temple libraries also served as state archives and public libraries (Affleck 2013). It has been estimated that the average temple and priestly collections in the Roman period contained about 20,000 to 40,000 papyrus rolls (Harris 1999, 64). There are a few physical remains of pagan libraries from the classical era;[1] the references in literature are usually the only clues to their existence. After the decline of the Western Roman Empire in the 5th century AD, Roman pagan temple collections were either destroyed by the barbarians and Christians or decayed as a result of neglect and disuse.

The later part of the Roman Empire saw the beginning of Christian libraries (see Humphreys 2013), the most notable of which was the library of Caesarea in Palestine, which, with its 30,000 volumes, was the largest ecclesiastical library in late antiquity. There is not so much information about pre-medieval Christian libraries in Europe because of the strong persecution of Christians at the time, especially by the emperor Diocletian. It is known that Pope Damasus (366–384 AD) organized a repository of the Church archives in Rome in the Church of St. Laurent. Most other early European Christian libraries were probably in the possession of theologians and monastic communities spread across Southern Europe.

Before Western Europe was overrun by the barbarians, the center of European culture moved in the 4th century from Rome to Constantinople and the Eastern Roman Empire, which assured the preservation of classical literature through the Middle Ages. Byzantium was known for its large imperial and university library in Constantinople and also patriarchal and numerous Christian monastic libraries (see Allison 2013; Schreiner 2013). Some of the most notable Byzantine monastic libraries, which are still operating, are the libraries on Holy Mount Athos in Greece and the Library of the Monastery of St. Catharine at Mount Sinai in Egypt, which, with its 1,500-year history, is reported to be the world's oldest continually operating library (Esparza 2019). The significance of Byzantine libraries for European librarianship is that they preserved much of the classical literature when it was virtually lost in the West (Harris 1999, 76). Both Byzantine and Islamic libraries served as a connecting link between the classical world and later European cultural development in the Renaissance.

Islamic libraries (see Wilkins 2013; Abattouy 2012; Gianni 2016) influenced European libraries particularly through their presence in the Iberian Peninsula and Sicily, which became the major centers of transmission of Arabic and classical knowledge and culture to medieval Europe. From 711, when Moslems entered Spain, until 1492, when they were expelled by Christians, Islamic libraries in Spain were the richest and most advanced libraries on the European continent. The most known among these is the Royal Library in Córdoba, which had approximately 400,000–600,000 volumes in the 10th century and employed 500 people. In addition to the Royal Library, Spain was also home to numerous university and public libraries as well as libraries of mosques (BenAicha 1986). Islamic libraries have contributed significantly to transmitting works of Greek, Persian, Indian, and Assyrian physicians and philosophers, which were later translated into Latin and used as textbooks in European schools at Bologna, Naples, and Paris (Algeriani and Mohadi 2017). Some European universities, like the University of Salamanca, were later modeled on the "houses of wisdom" found in the Muslim world (Harris 1999, 85). Jewish libraries (see Schidorsky 2013) were also present in Arabic Spain and, most especially, in Italy in the early Middle Ages. When Christians reconquered Spain in 1492, Moors and Jews were expelled and most of their literary heritage was either destroyed or taken by their owners.

During the 1000-year period in which Byzantine and Islamic libraries represented major centers of learning, Christian medieval monastic libraries (see McCrank 2013), particularly of the Benedictine, Cistercian, and Carthusian orders, kept the fire of learning in Central and Western Europe. The monks diligently copied and guarded their small collections of manuscripts and codices throughout the early middle ages. Italian monasteries were known for translating Byzantine texts, while monks in Muslim/Christian border areas in Spain and Sicily copied the contents of Islamic libraries and later spread them into other parts of Christian Europe. Some of these monastic libraries, such as the abbey library in St. Gall in Switzerland, still exist today.

Later, in the 12th century, when European social and intellectual life was moving more to the cities under the influence of trade, church and cathedral libraries (see Humphreys 2013) became a more prominent form of theological library. Although they were never as numerous as those of the monasteries and not as important in the preservation of the cultural history of Western Europe, they served as a bridge, chronologically and culturally, between the monasteries and the universities (Harris 1999, 98). Many prominent European universities, such as the University of Paris, were an outgrowth of cathedral schools that existed previously in these cities.

Although individual collections of medieval monastic and cathedral libraries remained relatively small, by the time of the Renaissance their network had grown very strong. With the growth of the universities during the 13th and 14th centuries, and especially after the invention of the printing press in the 15th century, monastic and cathedral libraries were replaced by university libraries as primary centers of learning in Europe. Because of the long heritage of literary production and because theological studies was one of the main disciplines at the time, collections in religion and theology represented the largest part of early university libraries.

During the period of the Renaissance (roughly from the 14th into the 17th century) the libraries of the monasteries, cathedrals, and theological faculties continued to exist, but their collections did not grow as much as the private libraries of the humanists, princes, and cardinals who competed to have the best collections of Greek and Latin doctors and philosophers. It was in the Renaissance that the Vatican Library was formally established and began to collect a whole universe of knowledge. The Renaissance was also a time of great religious turmoil and changes, culminating in the Protestant Reformation and Catholic Counter-Reformation, which had deep effects on theological libraries across Europe.

*Image 1: The Baroque Hall of the Abbey Library of St. Gall in Switzerland © Erwin Reiter, Haslach, Germany*

After the 16th century and into the period of the Enlightenment, the overall position and development of theological libraries were greatly influenced and affected by religious wars, censorship, and waves of secularizations that led their collections to be confiscated, suppressed, scattered, or destroyed.

The first of these waves of secularization came with the Reformation and religious wars connected with it. Many monastic and cathedral libraries were either destroyed or saw their collections confiscated and given to royal treasuries, aristocratic courts, wealthy cities, universities, certain individuals, and the new Protestant clerical order (Garrett 2015, 61). The second wave of secularization occurred in the 18th century and affected mostly Catholic Europe, but later spread all over Europe in the French Revolution and Napoleonic wars. During the period of cancellation of the Jesuit order (1773–1814), the Josephine reforms in the Habsburg lands (1773–1855; see Buchmayr 2004), secularizations in German states, and the partitions of Poland in the 19th century, numerous monastic libraries disappeared in Central Europe. Their holdings were confiscated and later mostly used for the development of national libraries. The cultural impact of the second wave of secularization was much greater than the first because 300 years of the printing press had, in the meantime, caused a large increase of theological library collections. After the second wave, the European library landscape and knowledge culture dramatically changed. Huge state-owned collections and smaller regional and university libraries with increasing relevance for science started to appear, creating a knowledge infrastructure that remained for the next 200 years (Garrett 2015, 61).

Waves of secularizations continued to affect theological libraries in the 20th century. In some countries, like France, laws on the separation of church and state were introduced. The status of the Church and its institutions, such as theological faculties, became private, and theological libraries could not count on receiving support from the government for their work. In the First and Second World War, many theological libraries were destroyed. Two of the best-known examples are the burning of the Central Library of the Catholic University of Leuven in Belgium in 1914 and 1940, and book-burnings and libricides before and during World War II by the Nazis, where most Jewish libraries in Europe were confiscated, destroyed, and scattered (see Sutter 2004; Rose 2008; Glickman 2016). It has been estimated that, before the war, the Jewish libraries in Germany and its occupied territories held four million volumes. Only two million of them were retrieved after the war (Schidorsky 2013). After the world wars, communist regimes came to power in Central and Eastern Europe. Where theological libraries were not confiscated, damaged, or robbed, access to them was restricted and tightly controlled. The communists did not allow expansion of theological studies and their libraries, so the collections, including the precious old historical manuscripts, were neglected for almost five decades. It was only after the fall of the communist regimes in 1989 that theological libraries in most Eastern European countries began to revive. The only exception to this is the libraries in the countries of Southeastern Europe, where the breakup of Yugoslavia resulted in a series of wars and ethnic cleansing that lasted for most of the 1990s. During the fights for territories, many Catholic, Orthodox, and Muslim libraries were destroyed in Bosnia and Herzegovina, Croatia, and Kosovo in an attempt to obliterate evidence of faith, culture, and memory of people of the different ethnic and religious traditions that lived in these parts (Brailo 1998; Riedlmayer 2008; Battles 2015, 99).

During the second half of the 20th century, church membership in Central and Western Europe across denominations dropped remarkably and, together with it, religious vocations. Many churches, abbeys, and cloisters were closed down.

Parallel to the decrease in church membership, Western Europe has been facing a strong influx of immigrants of Christians, Muslims, and other religions from all over the world, which is leading to a change of its religious landscape. Non-believers and adherents to a new spirituality, esoteric movements, and others are also increasing.

Amid these great challenges and changes in the social and political environment affecting churches and their libraries in the 20th century, an important change happened in the Catholic Church with the Second Vatican Council (1962-1965). Vatican II changed many things in the way the Catholic Church considers itself in dialogue with society, which includes also the role played by libraries. Before Vatican II, theological faculties and libraries did not cooperate very much, and the presence of lay people working in them was marginal. After the Council, many European theological libraries moved from purely ecclesial management of libraries that lacked professionalism to management by trained laypeople. In this period, many professional library associations began forming in Europe and their influence on theological library development has been significant ever since.

Since Vatican II, there has been more focus on the protection of church cultural heritage across denominations from the side of popes, bishops, and other church leaders. Pope John Paul II was especially instrumental in this regard and created the Pontifical Commission for the Cultural Patrimony of the Church in 1988. The Commission has, since its founding, issued several documents, among which the most relevant for libraries were guidelines titled *Ecclesiastical Libraries and Their Role in the Mission of the Church*, published in 1994, and the *Circular Letter on the Necessity and Urgency of the Inventory and Cataloging of the Church's Cultural Heritage*, published in 1999. Pope John Paul II also referred to church libraries in his apostolic constitution *Pastor bonus* (1988, art. 101, §1-2), as has Pope Francis in the apostolic constitution *Veritatis gaudium* (2018).

Many other church leaders across denominations were actively involved in developing theological library associations and centers for the protection of religious heritage and documentation in their countries.[2] Some Catholic bishops' conferences, such as in Bosnia and Hercegovina (BK BiH 2019) and Croatia (HBK 2001), as well as the Church of England in the UK (Church of England n.d.) have issued guidelines for church libraries. In the Reformed Church in Hungary, there is a responsible body called ORGYT (Országos Református Gyűjteményi Tanács) and a network of clerical members responsible for the preservation of the Hungarian Reformed heritage.

# Current Status

It has been estimated that there are around 3,000 active theological libraries on the European continent today, with total holdings of around 100 million–often very valuable collections (Geuns 2000, 232). These libraries can be divided into two basic categories. The first are those that directly belong to and serve religious institutions (libraries of churches, mosques, and synagogues, religious orders, monastic and diocesan institutions, and ecclesiastical universities, seminaries, and faculties). The second are libraries oriented toward a wider public and not directly linked to any particular religious organization, such as libraries which are part of public universities, or information and documentation centers. According to Geuns (2000, 238), neither ecclesiastical nor secular theological libraries today have a majority on the European continent.

When it comes to state recognition, most of the laws on libraries in European countries do not mention theological, church, or religious libraries, except for the library laws of three German federal states[3] and Hungary.[4] They are also usually not included in the national library statistics or directories as a special category. Academic theological libraries are included in these directories as school or academic libraries, while those belonging to churches, mosques, and synagogues and their institutions (parish, diocesan, monastic) are usually ignored. But the most important religions and denominations in all European countries, e.g. Catholic, Jewish, Orthodox, Muslim, Protestant, are recognized as religions with everything they represent; thus, also libraries. Most European countries have agreements or conventions with various religious communities, such as concordats with the Holy See. In these agreements, the state usually promises to support the work of religious communities and their institutions by allocating a certain amount from the annual budget. Some countries, such as Italy, have special agreements only on archives and libraries (ABEI, n.d.). Although these types of agreements do not specify any fixed sums theological libraries can count on every year, their existence is very important because it confirms the interest of the state in supporting religious libraries and allows their participation in the local library community.

Generally, European theological libraries receive funding through the institution to which they belong (school, university, diocese, religious order). Many European academic theological libraries are part of the public university system and receive funding from the state budget. Where they are not part of the public system, they can always ask for support and apply for donations. Monastic, church, mosque, and synagogue libraries usually do not receive any direct funding from the state, unless they have significant historical value or are located in nice historical buildings. Then they receive government support for

*Image 2: Archbishop's Diocesan and Cathedral Library in Cologne, Germany © [Pit Siebigs, Aachen] / Diözesan- und Dombibliothek Köln*

preservation and restoration. In countries such as France, where there is a strict separation of church and state, theological libraries cannot receive funds as theological libraries; they have to be organizations outside of the church. However, sometimes a theological library can receive grants for a particular project for which a public library or an institution has an interest (conversion of catalogs, digitization of collections, etc.).

European theological libraries are more open today to work with each other. This trend has increased even more since the 1990s and computerization in the libraries. They are cooperating with national, professional, ecumenical, and denominational networks to make their collections visible. The majority of European countries have a national catalog and, within them, one can search for theological collections and resources mostly coming from theology faculty libraries. In addition, there are three joint catalogs of religious literature in Europe organized by theological library associations–VThK in Germany, UNITAS in Hungary, and FIDES in Poland–which also bring religious heritage from their smaller church libraries into the internet. Index Theologicus (IxTheo) is an international scientific open access bibliography for theology and religious studies maintained by the university library in Tübingen in cooperation with the

Protestant and Catholic faculty of the same university and supported by the German Research Foundation (DFG). With over two million titles, it is the largest free open source bibliography of theological publications in Europe. The same university library maintains another bibliography specifically for religious studies called RelBib. Records from IxTheo are included in the Global Digital Library on Theology and Ecumenism (GlobeTheoLib), as of 2019 integrated into *Globethics .net*, a project of the World Council of Churches, which brings together resources on applied ethics, education, and religious studies from all over the world.

On a Christian denominational level, the libraries of the five Catholic universities in France–Paris, Lille, Lyon, Angers, and Toulouse–had built the portal Origène through their association (UDESCA), and the French Protestant libraries have been working in their union catalog Valdo. The rich heritage of Italian Catholic ecclesiastical libraries is made available through a cross portal, BeWeb. Monastic libraries have also joined forces to present their resources to the public. There are joint catalogs of Dominicans in Poland (*http://biblio .dominikanie.pl/*), and Benedictines and Trappists in Flanders and the Netherlands (*http://www.monasteria.org/wab/*).

When it comes to non-Christian libraries, a large initiative has been taken by several Jewish libraries in France, which in 2004 launched their union catalog and network called Rachel, which has close to 200,000 bibliographic records and is integrated into major French union catalogs. Rachel aspires to become a Europe-wide consortium in the future and a key tool for bibliographic research in Jewish studies (Musnik 2014). Another important project related to Jewish heritage is Judaica Europeana, which is a network of archives, libraries, and museums from Europe, Israel, and the USA working together to integrate access to the most important collections of European Jewish heritage and make it available in Europeana (Winer 2014). To date, Judaica Europeana has integrated collections from 25 institutions in Europe, Israel, and the US. Among partner institutions are the most important Judaica collections in Europe, such as the Bibliotheca Rosenthaliana of the University of Amsterdam, the Judaica Collection of the Frankfurt University Library, and the Jewish Historical Institute in Warsaw. The Frankfurt Judaica Collection houses the most comprehensive historical collection of Jewish literature in Germany and is the responsible library for providing information services on Jewish studies (Fachinformationsdienst Jüdische Studien) on a German level. The library maintains a search portal (*Jewishstudies .de*) which gives central access to electronic and printed books and periodicals, as well as databases in the entire spectrum of Jewish and Israel Studies. Poland is also home to three catalogs and databases on Jewish studies. The first is called Centralna Biblioteka Judaistyczna [Central Jewish Library] and is a repository of digitized Judaica housed by the Emanuel Ringelblum Jewish Historical Institute in Warsaw and other archives in Poland. The other two projects are created and maintained by the Institute of Jewish Studies at Jagiellonian University. The first is called Judaica: Online Catalogue of the Materials on the History and Culture of the Polish Jews, and is concerned with Jewish history and culture listed in the inventories of Małopolska regional libraries and archives. The second is a database on Jewish self-government in Poland in the 17th–18th century. JudaicaLink is another European project which provides support to publish and interlink existing reference works of Jewish culture and history (encyclopedia, glossaries, and library catalogs) as linked data.

As for Islamic libraries in Europe, Germany is home to the MENALIB Virtual Library, which provides central access to the holdings, offerings, and services of the Specialized Information Service (FID) for Middle East-, North Africa- and Islamic Studies. As is the case with the IxTheo, RelBib, and *Judaica.de* portals, MENALIB is also funded by the German Research Foundation (DFG). The portal has been maintained since 2016 by the University and State Library of Saxony-Anhalt in Halle. Many big and important German and European libraries and museums that possess Islamic collections contribute and partner with MENALIB. In the UK, Oxford and Cambridge University libraries have launched a free online catalog for Islamic manuscript descriptions called FIHRIST, which provides entries on Islamic manuscripts from all subject areas and of various geographical origins dating from the 7th to the 19th centuries now located in UK libraries. Cambridge University is also home to the Sunna Project, which aims to assemble the entirety of hadith literature and to prepare and publish definitive critical editions of every hadith collection. The Sunna Project is affiliated with the Prince Alwaleed Bin Talal Centre of Islamic Studies, University of Cambridge, and supported by the Thesaurus Islamicus Foundation.

When it comes to Buddhist collections in Europe, the field is almost completely unresearched. The only research which can be found is on Buddhist libraries in the UK. Carlos Garcia-Jane (2015) identifies and describes 31 UK Buddhist libraries, most of which are monastic (11) and located in London and the surrounding areas. Most Buddhist libraries in the UK have between 2,000 and 4,000 books, with two holding over 15,000 items: Christmas Humphreys Memorial Library and the library of the Centre for Applied Buddhism.

## European Theological Education and Libraries

As was mentioned in the first chapter, the first European higher education institutions and their libraries were founded based on Islamic Houses of Wisdom and Christian monastery and cathedral schools of late antiquity and the early

Middle Ages. Universities, as a form of higher education, emerged from them during the Middle Ages (11th to 13th century), gradually expanding and moving out of the Christian community. Under the influence of the Enlightenment, the Napoleonic organization of states, and Humboldt's educational reform, modern research universities and colleges took shape at the turn of the 18th and 19th centuries, and their founding and operation has since become fully governed by national higher education laws (Gallifa and Gassiot 2012). Many universities across Europe, and with them faculties of theology, became state property at that time, especially in those countries where the Napoleonic influence was important (Stewart 2001). With the growth of modern universities, the academy and higher education have been characterized since the 19th century by an ever-increasing deconfessionalization, professionalization, and specialization of study programs (Howard 2006, 11). Theology as a subject lost its medieval epithet as the "queen of sciences," and theological faculties their formerly exalted and privileged status in the academy. Many distinguished representatives of the Enlightenment thought at the time that theology had no place at the university (Howard 2006, 2–4). As a result, many dioceses, religious orders, and certain religious communities began, during the 19th and 20th centuries, to open new private colleges and universities across Europe for the purpose of renewing religious (Christian) higher education. For example, there are approximately 50 Catholic universities in Europe today, offering degrees in theology and other study disciplines.

Because of all these changes in the social and political environment and higher education system, the context in which European theological higher education institutions and their libraries are located and operating today is a very complex reality. To begin with, theological studies can be found in public universities as an academic discipline in its own right and also tied to a particular denomination–usually Catholic or Protestant. The first usually do not have any formal affiliation to any particular church and do not focus on ministerial training. This is the case, for instance, in many university departments in the UK, including the Faculty of Divinity at the University of Cambridge. The second focus more on ministerial training and offer denominationally-bound degrees. Such is the case at many German and Scandinavian universities, as well as theological faculties in former communist countries which were again incorporated into public universities after the fall of their regimes. Next, there are studies in theology at private universities, colleges, and seminaries that are almost always founded by and affiliated with a particular religious community. Here belong all ecclesiastical, pontifical and Catholic universities, for example, as well as seminaries of different Protestant denominations. Lastly, there are also religious studies programs, which are offered sometimes in combination with theological studies or separately at both state and private universities.

Image 3: Maurits Sabbe Library of the Faculty of Theology and Religious Studies, Catholic University in Leuven, Belgium © [Erfgoedcel Leuven] / Maurits Sabbe Library

The *Global Directory of Theological Education Institutions* lists 1,288 institutions in Europe that offer theological education. The changes in the social environment, secularization, and decreasing numbers of students in the last 50 years, as well as changes in the higher education systems (such as the Bologna process and digitalization) have encouraged the centralization and fusion of theological colleges in Europe. In many (particularly Western) European countries, smaller seminaries were integrated into bigger faculties and universities. Although most theological faculty libraries belonging to public universities still have theological collections organized in special branch libraries, in some countries, at bigger universities, theological collections are now being further integrated into the main university libraries. This is particularly the case in Finland, which about ten years ago began a large initiative of merging independent higher education institutions, their libraries, and research centers into larger units, funded no more by the government but through foundations that would take charge of certain universities (Haavisto 2009, 5). In other parts of Europe integration of libraries has been mostly happening on a virtual level, where smaller independent seminaries and their theological libraries are joining the university digital networks.

The state of library collections in these schools varies, of course, from one state to another, and depends on whether they are part of a public or private university, which determines the level of financial support they can count on. Generally, those libraries within a college of a religious community are naturally focused on collecting material from their spiritual tradition, while public-sector libraries at universities, especially if they have religious studies programs attached to theology, are required to provide material from different spiritual traditions.

Access to electronic publications and digital databases is especially important for academic theological libraries nowadays. In Europe, libraries are using a variety of means to access these resources: individually or in cooperation with other libraries in the form of national or subject-specific consortia. Many European countries also have agencies that negotiate licenses on a national level.

In the context of legal deposit, there are certain libraries in some European countries that have been mandated to collect religious literature published in the country, as well as large parts of theological publications in native languages from other countries. Thus, in Germany, the area of religion was assigned to the library of the University of Tübingen, in France to the National Library in Strasbourg, in Poland to the Catholic University of Lublin, and in the United Kingdom to the library of the University of Oxford. This policy is still very useful as it significantly contributes to the possibility of making a wide selection of theological literature available to more users (Geuns 2000, 238).

Open access is another important topic in European academic and research libraries. More and more governments are supporting open access and requiring that state-funded research be made available in institutional and open repositories. Some countries, like the Netherlands, are planning to make all their scientific publications available through open access by 2024 (Blin 2017). Academic theological libraries in Europe support open access and are involved in the creation of many repositories, databases, and digital libraries, which they publish individually or in cooperation with their national theological library associations and societies. The most notable example is the IxTheo database from the university library in Tübingen, which also hosts some open journals.

## Library Education Programs

In Europe, as in most countries today, higher education (HE) is considered as a basic path for the education of librarians. Library and information science (LIS) study programs in Europe are part of the European Higher Education Area (EHEA), which is the result of the Bologna Process–a series of ministerial meetings, agreements, and reforms started in 1999 between European countries with the goal of ensuring comparability and compatibility in the standards and quality of higher-education qualifications. HE programs in the EHEA are offered at three levels–undergraduate, graduate, and doctoral studies–which are usually referred to as the 'three-cycle system.'

Today there is a broad range of bachelor's, master's, and doctoral programs in LIS being offered across Europe (see Schniederjürgen 2007). According to Àngel Borrego (2015), there are 220 centers offering LIS education in 26 EU countries. Programs are offered at undergraduate, graduate, and doctoral levels, although there is a higher tendency to offer bachelor's degrees. Italy and France have the largest number of institutions offering LIS-related programs. Most LIS education institutions function as a unit or department within a specific host faculty or as a program within a particular department. Also, a growing trend has been observed for LIS academic institutions to transform themselves into iSchools (Horvat, Kajberg, Oguz, and Tammaro 2017, 7). As for the curriculum structure and orientation, Borrego concludes that there is no common European approach to LIS education. The number and disciplinary orientation of LIS-related centers vary widely from country to country.

There are two principal routes which one can take toward professional library qualification in Europe at the moment: an undergraduate LIS degree as the first route or a master's degree coupled with a first degree in some other discipline as the second route (Horvat, Kajberg, Oguz, and Tammaro 2017, 17). In some countries, like Germany, the second route is necessary if one wants to be employed at a higher grade of service (*höherer Dienst*). After finishing formal studies there is usually no certification or license procedure that needs to be passed. Having a degree is considered as a qualification. However, in some Central and Southern European countries, like Slovakia and Croatia, librarians need to pass a state exam at the end of their program in order to receive a formal qualification from the state and also compete for jobs in state-funded libraries.

Having a formal degree in library science is not mandatory to receive a job in a theological or any other library in Europe today. Library boards in religion-related institutions usually do not oblige candidates to have an LIS degree. Theological libraries mainly hire theologians to work in their libraries. Also, for certain departments, like acquisitions, special collections, or technical services, a degree in history or computing science may be more favorable than a degree in librarianship.

## Continuing Education and Professional Development Opportunities

In most European countries there is a wide palette of various continuing professional activities and programs on a national and provincial level targeted at all kinds of library workers and libraries. These programs are usually conducted by national libraries or national library associations, as well as specialized training centers and companies formed in cooperation with LIS schools and other related institutions.

When it comes to professional development opportunities specifically targeted for theological librarians in Europe, there are two continuing education programs, one in Germany and another in Italy, both intended for non-professional staff working in church libraries and organized by their national theological library associations. The program in Germany is organized by the Association of Ecclesiastical Libraries in the Evangelical Church (Verband kirchlich-wissenschaftlicher Bibliotheken–VkwB) and is divided into three modules: Basic course 1 and 2, and an Advanced course. The first two modules cover basic LIS topics such as formal and subject cataloging, information literacy and conservation, as well as public relations and the book trade. The advanced module offers more information about information literacy and copyright. The program is delivered in the form of one-week or 36-hour courses once a year at different locations in Germany and is available to all librarians regardless of confession. The second program in Italy is a new program started in October 2019. It is organized by the Italian Association of Ecclesiastical Libraries (ABEI) in cooperation with the Pontifical University Gregoriana and the National Office for Ecclesiastical Cultural Heritage of the Italian Bishop's Conference (CEI). The program is divided into four modules: understanding the organization of the regional ecclesiastical network, protection and preservation, and back- and front-office library activities and tasks. It is delivered during a span of one year in the form of classes held at the Pontifical Gregorian University. Both associations have also organized introductory and advanced courses on the RDA cataloging rules.

Another training opportunity, where theological librarians can also participate, is organized by the Research Infrastructure on Religious Studies (ReIReS) project. ReIReS is an EU-funded project whose aim is to build a research infrastructure on religious studies by offering various research activities and transnational and virtual access to the most significant tools and sources in the field of religious studies. As part of its work, ReIReS offers six week-long schools on the use and study of special documents and also six three-day courses on digital humanities and historical religious studies at the project's partner institutions across Europe.

Other continuing education opportunities for theological librarians are usually combined with the annual conferences of theological library associations. Some associations and special committees within them, like in Germany (the *Altbestandskommission* of the AKThB and VkwB) and Hungary (the Hungarian Association of Ecclesiastical Libraries, or EKE), also organize special professional events and courses during the year where renowned speakers are invited to talk about topics related to general and theological librarianship. Sometimes these events are organized in cooperation with national library associations and other cultural and heritage institutions.

There are also two events for European monastic libraries. The first is a conference series called *Fachtage für Klosterkultur* (Professional Days for Monastic Culture) organized by the Abbey Library of St. Gall in Switzerland and the monastery and National Museum for Monastic Culture in Dalheim, Germany. The conferences take place at intervals of two years alternately in the Abbey of St. Gall and the monastery at Dalheim. The other event for monastic libraries is organized by the group of Benedictine and Trappist abbeys and various seminars in Flanders and the Netherlands called the Werkgroep Abdij Bibliotheken (WAB). Members of WAB use the same library systems, called BIDOC, and have annual events related to cataloging and working in this system.

On a European level, there is also an Erasmus+ exchange training program for staff. In this program, European librarians can spend a short time working in a library located in another European country and learn about their library practice and tradition. Theological librarians who work in institutions that are part of the Erasmus+ National Mobility Consortium can use this opportunity. Exchange programs for theological librarians have also been offered by the Maurits Sabbe Library in Leuven, Belgium. Also, many theological libraries around Europe frequently have guest students or library workers from Europe and all over the world visiting their libraries.

## European Theological Library Associations

The earliest attempt at forming an autonomous association of theological libraries in Europe took place in Germany in 1947, when the Association of Catholic Theological Libraries (*Arbeitsgemeinschaft Katholisch-Theologischer Bibliotheken*, or AKThB) was founded. Soon after, similar associations of predominantly Catholic libraries were formed in other European countries (the UK, Netherlands, France, and Belgium) gradually growing into a federated body in 1961 called the International Committee for the Co-ordination of the Associations of Libraries of Catholic Theology (CIC). After the Second Vatican

Council, the CIC began to expand more into the ecumenical sphere and changed its name to the International Council of Theological Library Associations (*le Conseil international des associations de bibliothèques de théologie*). New statutes were adopted in a meeting held on 26 September 1973, and the association received royal approval in the Netherlands. In 1999, the Council, in order to emphasize the specifically European character of its activities, changed the name of the association into BETH: *Bibliothèques Européennes de Théologie* / European Theological Libraries / *Europäische Bibliotheken für Theologie*.

## BETH

Today, BETH is an ecumenical federation of European national theological library societies based in the Netherlands. It brings together around 1,500 theological libraries across Europe with an estimated stock of more than 60 million volumes and an important collection of ancient manuscripts. Its purpose is to encourage the development and cooperation of theological and religious libraries on the European continent. The membership of BETH is divided into ordinary and extraordinary members. Ordinary members are different national theological library associations. Extraordinary members are individual theological libraries. Each year, BETH organizes a general assembly in one of the European countries on topics relevant to European theological librarianship.

## Library Associations by Country

In addition to BETH, there are a total of twenty theological library associations in Europe. Most of them (14) are represented in BETH as ordinary members.

As can be seen from the below table, some countries, like France, Germany, Italy, and the UK, have more than one theological library association. They are usually divided along denominational lines, but there are exceptions, such as in Italy with the ABEI and URBE. URBE is predominantly an association of ecclesiastical universities in Rome and the Vatican, while the ABEI is an association that represents mainly ecclesiastical libraries across Italy. Both associations share some of the same members.

Most of the European theological library associations are autonomous associations, with defined statutes and organizational structure. Some, like the Catholic associations in Belgium, France, Germany, Italy, Poland, and Spain, are officially recognized by their national bishops' conferences.

The membership in most associations comes from various theological libraries in their own countries: academic, diocesan, monastic, etc. Some, such as the German AKThB, have members outside of their borders. The AKThB's members come from all the German-speaking countries (Austria, Germany, and Switzerland) but also from Italy, Luxembourg, Denmark, and Hungary.

| Country | Association | Religious Affiliation | Year of Foundation |
|---|---|---|---|
| Belgium | Expertisehouders Levensbeschouweliike Collecties (VRB) | Mainly Roman Catholic, but open to all denominations | 1965 |
| Finland | Suomen teologinen kiriastoseura (STK) | / | 2017 |
| France | Association des Bibliotheques Chretiennes de France (ABCF) | Mainly Roman Catholic, but open to all denominations | 1957 |
| | Rachel — Le Réseau des bibliotheques europeen judaica et hebraica (REBJH) | / | 2004 |
| | Réseau VALDO | Protestant | 2008 |
| Germany | Arbeitsgemeinschaft Katholisch-Theologischer Bibliotheken (AKThB) | Roman Catholic | 1947 |
| | Verband kirchlich-wissenschaftlicher Bibliotheken in der Arbeitsgemeinschaft der Archive and Bibliotheken in der evangelischen Kirche (VkwB) | Protestant | 1936, 1980 |
| Hungary | Egyhazy Konyvtarak Egyestilese (EKE) | Ecumenical & Interreligious | 1994 |
| Italy | Associazione dei Bibliotecari Eccliesiastici Italiani (ABEI) | Roman Catholic | 1978 |
| | Unione Romana Biblioteche Ecclesiastiche (URBE) | Roman Catholic | 1974 |
| Netherlands | Vereniging voor het Theologisch Bibliothecariaat (VThB) | Ecumenical & Interreligious | 1947 |
| Norway | Forum for teologiske og religionsfaglige bibliotek (FTRB) | / | 1972 |
| Poland | Federacia Bibliotek Kokielnych „Fides" (FIDES) | Roman Catholic | 1991 |
| Spain | Asociacion de Bibliotecarios de la Iglesia en Espana (ABIE) | Roman Catholic | 1993 |
| Switzerland | Verein der Bibliothekarinnen religionsbezogener Institutionen der Schweiz (BibRel.ch) | Ecumenical & Interreligious | 2016 |
| UK | Christian Librarian's Fellowship (CLIS) | Protestant | 1973 |
| | The Islamic Manuscript Association (TIMA) | / | 2006 |
| | European Association of Middle East Librarians (MELCom) | / | 1967 |
| UK & Ireland | Association of British Theological and Philosophical Libraries (ABTAPL) | Open to all types of theological and philosophical libraries | 1956 |
| | The Cathedral Archives, Libraries and Collections Association (CALCA) | Anglican | 1975 |

*Table 1: European Theological Library Associations by Country*

## Projects and Activities

European theological library associations are involved in numerous projects and activities. The majority of them organize annual conferences, alone or together with other library associations in the country or across borders. For example, the two German associations–AKThB and VkwB–organize a joint conference every three years, as do the Flemish VRB and Dutch VThB every couple of years. Some associations, like the Italian ABEI, organize conferences often in cooperation with the Italian Library Association (ABI).

Also, almost all of the associations publish some type of publication: bulletin, newsletter, journal, yearbook, bibliographies, summaries of proceedings from conferences, and different monographs and booklets about the association or theological libraries in their countries. Some publications are published annually (e.g. *ABCF Bulletin*), others, like in the UK, Italy, and Hungary, three to four times a year. Most of them are non-peer-reviewed publications, except for the Polish *Fides. Biuletyn Bibliotek Kościelnych* [Bulletin of Church Libraries] and *The Journal of Islamic Manuscripts* by the Islamic Manuscript Association (TIMA). Poland is also home to the oldest European journal of church archives, libraries, and museums *Archiwa, Biblioteki i Muzea Kościelne* [Ecclesiastical Archives, Libraries and Museums], which has been published continuously since 1959.

When it comes to the organization of different projects, German, Hungarian, and Polish associations are the most active. Two German associations have three joint committees (Old prints and manuscripts, Church academic libraries, Church document repository–Kidoks), an interlibrary borrowing program, and several joint databases, digital libraries, and repositories, including the meta catalog VThK. Hungarian EKE and Polish Fides are also involved in many projects, namely their joint catalogs UNITAS and Fides, as well as many specific repositories, digital libraries, and databases.

## IFLA SIG RELINDIAL

European theological library associations and libraries have also been involved in the creation of IFLA's special interest group Libraries in Dialogue (RELINDIAL) in 2012. RELINDIAL is a special group within IFLA which includes library associations, libraries, and research centers around the world that are involved in serving and fostering interfaith dialogue between cultures through a better knowledge of religions. The project was initiated in 2009 at the IFLA annual conference in Italy and carried on for the next eight years by Odile Dupont, president of BETH from 2007-2012. In the last seven years, RELINDIAL has published (by itself or in association) several publications that present examples of libraries and library tools serving interreligious dialogue around the world. It has also launched a successful project called Relindial Cartonera, the aim of

Image 4: Members of BETH and the two German theological library associations, AKThB and VkwB, at their joint meeting in Heilsbronn in 2018. © [Susanne Hassen] / Evangelisches Sonntagsblatt aus Bayern

which is to help people, notably children, of different origins to learn about one another's religion by creating a Cartonera book together. Many European librarians and library associations were and are still involved in the work of RELINDIAL. It is hoped that the important work which has begun will continue successfully in the future.

## Challenges and Opportunities

Since the onset of the digital era, the place and relevance of libraries as information providers in society has been generally challenged. In addition to some traditional and new challenges European libraries are facing at the beginning of the 21st century, such as the reduction of funds because of successive economic crises and growing costs of electronic resources, digitalization, and digital transformation of science and copyright, there are some unique challenges affecting particularly theological libraries.

For academic theological libraries, the biggest problem is the decreasing number of students. The management of theological faculties is sometimes trying to cope with this trend by broadening the program offerings. In other places, faculties and programs are joined or integrated into other departments. All this brings further demands and pressures on libraries, particularly with acquisition, collection development, and staffing. Because of the decreasing number of students, there is overall an increasing reluctance from state and secular agencies and charities to provide grants to religious libraries for resources and projects, and many national agencies or big national consortia are often not interested in subscribing to relevant databases for theological studies.

The second biggest challenge for academic theological libraries is the divide that exists between theological libraries and librarians working in big publicly-funded universities and those in smaller, private, church-funded seminaries. Smaller libraries cannot compete with bigger libraries in terms of providing access to all electronic resources. On the other hand, bigger university libraries are more and more losing subject librarians specializing in theology, or they are responsible for more subjects, such as philosophy or history. Their workflow is often much different from the librarians working in smaller and private theological libraries. This divide poses many challenges for future cooperation.

For church and monastic libraries, closure, restoration of rare books, digitization, and long-term preservation are some of the main challenges. This has been especially challenging for libraries in former socialist countries, whose old collections were neglected for decades in the former regime. Many libraries there dream now of restoring and digitizing their precious rare books and manuscripts and making them available to the world, but very often there are no funds to be found which would support these projects.

Diocesan and cathedral libraries, which are also becoming less and less rich, share many of the same challenges as the church and monastic libraries, but their biggest difficulty is often the lack of interest and understanding of bishops and other church leaders for the protection of the church's cultural heritage.

However, in spite of all the effects of secularization, religion is still one of the major issues and topics in Europe's public sphere. The topic is even more enhanced in the last ten years as Europe is experiencing another strong wave of immigration from countries with different ethnic, religious, and cultural systems. This rise in attention to religious themes in the general public and society is a great opportunity for theological and religious libraries to make themselves more present, visible, and accessible. Although Europeans may not be generally attracted to visit churches to participate in the liturgy nowadays, they are still attracted to the buildings and cultural heritage.

*Image 5: Helsinki University Library with integrated collections in theology and religion.*
*© [Veikko Somerpuro] / Helsinki University Library*

As is the case with the popularization of churches in Europe, so it is with today's libraries. People are not primarily drawn to libraries to look for information anymore. Libraries are not their first choice; the internet is. Today, people come to the library most often for its programs or for a quiet place to work, alone or in study groups. In such a context, Simone Kortekaas (2019) advises that it is essential for all libraries to spread information about their holdings as broadly as possible, because if their records are not findable in Google and other search engines they won't be found. Similarly, if they are not available in a digitized way, they won't be read. Theological libraries need to make sure that, whatever library system they are using, the metadata is harvested by search engines. No library can rely anymore on the idea that people will come to their library website as a starting point for their research. In terms of digitization, if there is the possibility of digitization, theological libraries should digitize and give access to the full text. If they do not have enough budget for full digitization, they should at least describe their collections and make them findable for search engines. When it comes to collection development and acquisition, large university libraries are nowadays mostly buying big packages of electronic publications from important information providers and their collections are more and more looking the same. There is still an important part of literature which is outside of these packages, and this is an opportunity for smaller theological libraries to focus on purchasing those titles that are not provided by the big theological schools. There are so many rare and unique documents theological libraries can offer to today's researchers, and this information needs to become as available as it is possible.

For all of this to happen, theological libraries need to work more closely together. The concept of integration and cooperation has become of vital importance for all types of libraries today. Although European theological libraries and associations are involved in many networking and cooperative projects at the moment, there is a lot more work to be done on the European, but also international, level. In many European countries, particularly in Central and Eastern Europe, there is little cooperation between theological libraries because there are no library associations which would encourage it and advocate the interests of religious libraries in these countries. In Western and Northern Europe, there is often little cooperation between theological libraries belonging to large publicly-funded universities and smaller private seminary libraries (or even with one another). This weakens the whole branch of theological librarianship and its participation in today's culture. Therefore, it is essential that BETH and other European theological library associations and libraries actively engage themselves in unifying and fostering stronger cooperation between libraries regardless of their size and affiliation, as well as the type and nature of spiritual resources they are committed to protecting.

## Notes

1. Almost none for the Greek libraries, except the remains of the library at the Temple of Athena in Pergamum, which was also a famous royal, academic, and public library. One of the remains of Roman temple libraries is the Porticus Octaviae structure in Rome.
2. Many Catholic Bishops were instrumental in the founding of the Italian Association of Ecclesiastical Libraries–ABEI. In Belgium, Catholic bishops were included in the formation of the Center for Religious Art and Culture (CRKC) and the Documentation and Research Center for Religion, Culture and Society (KADOC).

3. Thüringer Bibliotheksrechtsgesetz § 1(6) (2008); Hessisches Bibliotheksgesetz. Wolters Kluwer Deutschland. § 3(1), § 5(1), § 8(4) (2010); Rheinland-Pfalz: Landesgesetz zum Erlass eines Bibliotheksgesetzes und zur Änderung und Aufhebung weiterer bibliotheksbezogenerer Vorschriften § 1(5) § 7(2) (2014).
4. Évi CXL. Törvény a muzeális intézményekről, a nyilvános könyvtári ellátásról és a közművelődésről. § 92(4) (1997).

## *Works Cited*

Abattouy, Mohammed. 2012. "The Arabic-Latin Intercultural Transmission of Scientific Knowledge in Pre-Modern Europe: Historical Context and Case Studies." In *The Role of the Arab-Islamic World in the Rise of the West: Implications for Contemporary Trans-Cultural Relations,* edited by Nayef R. F. Al-Rodhan, 167–219. Basingstoke: Palgrave Macmillan.

Affleck, Michael. 2013. "Priest, Patrons, and Playwrights: Libraries in Rome before 168 BC." In *Ancient Libraries,* edited by Jason König, 124–36. Cambridge: Cambridge University Press.

Algeriani, Adel and Mawloud Mohadi. 2017. "The House of Wisdom (Bayt al-Hikmah) and Its Civilizational Impact on Islamic libraries: A Historical Perspective." *Mediterranean Journal of Social Sciences* 8, no. 5 (September): 179–87. *http://www.doi.org/10.1515/mjss-2017-0036.*

Allison, Robert W. 2013. "Libraries: Eastern Christian." In *Encyclopedia of Monasticism,* edited by William M. Johnston, 757–65. Routledge.

Associazione dei Bibliotecari Ecclesiastici Italiani (ABEI). n.d. *Intesa Ministero Cei per archivi e biblioteche.* Accessed October 1, 2019, *http://www.abei.it/c/20 /Intesa_Ministero_Cei_per_archivi_e_biblioteche.html.*

Battles, Matthew. 2015. *Library: An Unquiet History.* New York: W. W. Norton & Company.

BenAicha, Hedi. 1986. "Mosques as Libraries in Islamic Civilization, 700–1400 A.D." *The Journal of Library History* 21, no. 2: 253–60.

Biskupska konferencija Bosne i Hercegovine (BK BiH). 2019. *Uredba BK BiH o crkvenim knjižnicama. http://www.bkbih.ba/info.php?id = 201.*

Blin, Frédéric. 2017. "Academic Libraries." In *Global Library and Information Science,* edited by Ismael Abdullahi, 467. Berlin and Boston: De Gruyter. *https: //doi.org/10.1515/9783110413120.*

Borrego, Àngel. 2015. "Library and Information Education in Europe: An Overview." *BiD: Textos Universitaris de Biblioteconomia i Documentació* 35 (December). *http://bid.ub.edu/en/35/borrego.htm.*

Brailo, Nensi. 1998. "Librocide: Destruction of Libraries in Croatia 1991–1995." Master's thesis, San Jose State University. *https://doi.org/10.31979/etd.zcc8–298e*.

Buchmayr, Friedrich. 2004. "Secularization and Monastic Libraries in Austria." In *Lost Libraries,* edited by James Raven, 145–162. London: Palgrave Macmillan.

Church of England. n.d. *Records Management Guides.* Accessed October 1, 2019, *https://www.churchofengland.org/more/libraries-and-archives/records-management-guides*.

Dupont, Odile and Christophe Langlois. 2011. "Les bibliothèques de théologie: interdisciplinarité et outils" [Theological Libraries: Interdisciplinarity and Tools]. Paper presented at the 77th IFLA General Conference and Assembly, San Juan, Puerto Rico. Accessed Oct 1, 2019, *https://www.ifla.org/past-wlic/2011/142-dupont-fr.pdf*.

Esparza, Daniel. 2019. "The Oldest Continuously Operating Library in the World is in This Egyptian Monastery." *Aleteia,* August 19. Accessed October 1, 2019, *https://aleteia.org/2019/08/19/the-oldest-continuously-operating-library-in-the-world-is-in-an-egyptian-monastery/*.

Francis I. 2018. *Veritatis gaudium. https://press.vatican.va/content/salastampa/en/bollettino/pubblico/2018/01/29/180129c.html*.

Gallifa, Josep and Miquel Gassiot. 2012. "Comparative Legal and Financial Situation of the European Catholic Universities." *Journal of Church and State* 54, no. 1: 84.

Garcia-Jane, Carlos. 2015. "Buddhist Libraries in the United Kingdom." Master's thesis, Aberystwyth University. *https://pure.aber.ac.uk/portal/files/28168271/Garcia_Jane_Carlos.pdf*.

Garrett, Jeffrey. 2015. "Klostersturm and Secularization in Central Europe: What Happened to the Libraries?" *Theological Librarianship* 8, no. 1: 61–9. *http://www.doi.org/10.31046/tl.v8i1.372*.

Geuns, André J. 2000. "From Ecclesiastic to Theological Libraries: How Religious Libraries Cope with Diversity in Europe." *American Theological Library Association Summary of Proceedings* 54: 229–42.

–––. 1999. "Past, Present, and Future of International Theological Librarianship: The European Experience." *American Theological Library Association Summary of Proceedings* 53: 247–52.

––– and Barbara Wolf-Dahm. 1998. "Theological Libraries: An Overview on History and Present Activities of the International Council of Associations of Theological Libraries." *INSPEL: International Journal of Special Libraries* 32, no. 3: 139–58.

Gianni, Celeste. 2016. *History of Libraries in the Islamic World: A Visual Guide.* Pesaro: Gimiano Editore.

Glickman, Mark. 2016. *Stolen Words: The Nazi Plunder of Jewish Books*. Lincoln: University of Nebraska Press.

Haavisto, Tuula. 2009. "Finland: Libraries, Museums and Archives in Finland." *https://www.libraries.fi/sites/default/files/content/finnishlibrarysystem.pdf*.

Harris, Michael H. 1999. *History of Libraries in the Western World*. Lanham, MD: The Scarecrow Press.

Horvat, Aleksandra, Leif Kajberg, Esin Oguz and Anna Maria Tammaro. 2017. "LIS Education." In *Global Library and Information Science*, edited by Ismael Abdullahi. Berlin and Boston: De Gruyter. *http://www.doi.org/10.1515/9783110413120–022*.

Howard, Thomas Albert. 2006. *Protestant Theology and the Making of the Modern German University*. Oxford: Oxford University Press.

Hrvatska biskupska konferencija (HBK). 2001. "Uredba HBK o crkvenim knjižnicama," *Vjesnik Đakovačke i Srijemske biskupije* 129.

Humphreys, Kenneth W. 2013. "Christian Libraries, Early." In *Encyclopedia of Library History*, edited by Wayne A. Wiegand, 138–39. New York: Taylor and Francis.

–––. 2013. "Church and Cathedral Libraries in Western Europe." In *Encyclopedia of Library History*, edited by Wayne A. Wiegand, 139–142. New York: Taylor and Francis.

John Paul II. 1988. *Pastor bonus*. *http://w2.vatican.va/content/john-paul-ii/en/apost_constitutions/documents/hf_jp-ii_apc_19880628_pastor-bonus.html*.

Kortekaas, Simone. 2019. "Access to Scientific Information Anyplace, Anytime, Anywhere." Presented at the 48th General Assembly of BETH, Oxford, September 7–11.

McCrank, Lawrence J. 2013. "Medieval Libraries." In *Encyclopedia of Library History*, edited by Wayne A. Wiegand, 420–31. New York: Taylor and Francis.

Murphy, Christopher. 2013. "Greece, Ancient." In *Encyclopedia of Library History*, edited by Wayne A. Wiegand, 249–50. New York: Taylor and Francis.

Musnik, Noémie. 2014. "Rachel: The Union Catalog of the European Network of Judaica and Hebraica Libraries." *Judaica Librarianship* 18: 116–129. *http://www.doi.org/10.14263/2330–2976.1020*.

Penner, Katharina. 2005. "Theological Libraries in Central and Eastern Europe." In *Theological Education as Mission*, edited by Peter F. Penner. Cuxhaven: Neufeld-Verlag. [Article reprinted in the 2005 *ANZTLA EJournal*: 2–13. *https://doi.org/10.31046/anztla.v0i58.1304*.]

Pontifical Commission for the Cultural Patrimony of the Church. 1999. *Lettera circolare Necessità e urgenza dell'inventariazione e catalogazione dei beni culturali della Chiesa*. http://www.vatican.va/roman_curia/pontifical _commissions/pcchc/documents/rc_com_pcchc_19991208_catalogazione-beni -culturali_it.html.

———. 1994. *Ecclesiastical Libraries and Their Role in the Mission of the Church*. http://www.vatican.va/roman_curia/pontifical_commissions/pcchc/documents /rc_com_pcchc_19940319_biblioteche-ecclesiastiche_en.html.

Riedlmayer, András. 2008. "Convivencia Under Fire: Genocide and Book Burning in Bosnia." In *The Holocaust and the Book: Destruction and Preservation*, edited by Jonathan Rose, 266–292. Amherst, MA: University of Massachusetts Press.

Rose, Jonathan. 2008. *The Holocaust and the Book: Destruction and Preservation*. Amherst, MA: University of Massachusetts Press.

Schidorsky, Dov. 2013. "Jewish Libraries." In *Encyclopedia of Library History*, edited by Wayne A. Wiegand, 325. New York: Taylor and Francis.

Schniederjürgen, Axel. 2007. *World Guide to Library, Archive and Information Science Education: Third New and Completely Revised Edition*. Berlin and Boston: K. G. Saur.

Schreiner, Peter. 2013. "Byzantine Libraries." In *Encyclopedia of Library History*, edited by Wayne A. Wiegand, 95–7. New York: Taylor and Francis.

Staikos, Konstantinos Sp. 2004–2013. *The History of the Library in Western Civilization*. Volumes I-VI. Leiden: Brill | Hes & De Graaf.

Stewart, David. 2001. "Christian Libraries." In *International Dictionary of Library Histories*, vol. 1, 52. Chicago: Fitzroy Dearborn Publishers.

Sutter, S. C. 2004. "The Lost Jewish Libraries of Vilna and the Frankfurt Institut zur Erforschung der Judenfrage." In *Lost Libraries*, edited by James Raven, 219–235. London: Palgrave Macmillan.

Wilkins, M. Lesley. 2013. "Islamic Libraries to 1920." In *Encyclopedia of Library History*, edited by Wayne A. Wiegand, 296–306. New York: Taylor and Francis.

Winer, Dov. 2014. "Judaica Europeana: An Infrastructure for Aggregating Jewish Content." *Judaica Librarianship* 18: 88–115. http://www.doi.org/10.14263 /2330–2976.1027.

# CHAPTER 6

# Theological Libraries in Eastern Europe and Central Asia

KATHARINA PENNER

## Introduction

Theological education and, with it, theological libraries on the territory of the former Soviet Union have experienced quite a varied history. This chapter will briefly present some of their beginnings and then attempt to describe the current state of theological libraries in the successor states. Usually, theological libraries in this part of the world, due to the Soviet heritage and the never-ending transitionary period, are relatively small and ill-resourced. Still, they are very aware of their calling to serve educational programs in theology and religion and strive to meet this challenge as best as they can. There are very few sources that deal with theological libraries in this region, and so the presentation will be sketchy at best. Many issues have been gleaned from personal interactions, which also leaves certain gaps in the overview as possibly not all important players have been recognized or contacted.

The presentation will proceed through five geographical regions, which comprise countries with a more or less similar cultural, religious, and educational background: 1) Russia and Belarus, 2) Ukraine, 3) Moldova, 4) Caucasus states (Georgia, Armenia, Azerbaijan), and 5) Central Asian states (Kazakhstan, Kyrgyzstan, Uzbekistan, Turkmenistan, Tajikistan). Such categorization also has its limitations and will lead to generalizations, which will hopefully not mar or distort the presentation of individual contextual situations. Where libraries of university faculties and/or national libraries comprise significant holdings relevant for theological studies and where these provide services for users of theological libraries they will also be included in the discussion. A summary of challenges that are common to theological libraries in this geographical region will conclude the presentation.

## The Russian Federation and Belarus

After the break-up of the Soviet Union, and after a short period of attempts at liberal democracy, institutions in both countries are exhibiting authoritarian tendencies. This has consequences for the practice of religion and for theological educational institutions, in terms of directives and regulations which the state imposes on their operations.[1] Libraries, including theological libraries, are also directly affected. For some time now, libraries in these countries have had to watch a blacklist of titles[2] that these governments consider dangerous and not permissible for circulation to patrons. So libraries have to restrict access, create special secure storage for these titles, or take them out of their holdings completely. Sometimes the reasons why these titles became blacklisted are not very obvious or reasoned. Usually, it is the attempt of the government to shield off radicalization of any kind or to impose top-down certain ethicist views or understandings of society. It is part of a larger set of activities to control public opinion and censor out the influence of unwelcome opinions. A climate of fear is created as librarians have to continuously watch the lists and are always in danger of jeopardizing their and their institutions' existence.

At the same time, there are also interesting developments in the academic world. After being carried out exclusively in the network of church seminaries and separated from the public university system, theology has received in 2015 the status of an accepted scientific discipline on public universities and theological education is now incorporated in the Russian state university system. At the moment, there are only curricula for studies in Orthodox, Islamic, and Buddhist theology. Christian theology, then, in the current legislation, is understood as Russian Orthodox theology, which severely limits Catholics, Lutherans, and the different Protestant denominations in teaching their confessional theology. At the time of writing, attempts are underway to develop curricula for Lutheran and other Protestant confessions.

The predominance of the Russian Orthodox Church has been obvious throughout previous centuries. This church first developed monasteries, which created and copied books, and seminaries as well as academies for priest training, which also had their own libraries. The libraries of the flagship academies in the Russian Empire just before the 1917 Revolution are cited to have had as many as 150,000 volumes and 4,116 manuscripts at the St. Petersburg Orthodox Academy and over 100,000 unique titles at the Moscow Orthodox Academy. The holdings comprised not only church and theological literature, but also significant collections in other disciplines, including *belles lettres* (fine literature, fiction). Most of it was confiscated during the Bolshevik Revolution, and only selective parts were returned when the academies were again able to restore their operations after the Second World War.

In Belarus, in Minsk, an Orthodox seminary was founded in 1785 and an Orthodox academy only in 1996, with the permission of Patriarch Alexiy II of Moscow. The library of the Orthodox Academy in Minsk has holdings of about 60,000 volumes, 7,000 of which are periodicals, and includes many unique manuscripts starting from the 16$^{th}$ century. The National Library of Belarus also has extensive theological holdings and maintains some historico-cultural religious interest by curating, for example, an exhibition on the Bible, or in January 2016 on Francysk Skaryna as Bible printer, or the 500$^{th}$ anniversary of the Reformation.

Orthodox theology is also taught at various other universities in Moscow, St. Petersburg, Kazan, and other cities. Holdings in theology are, in these cases, part of other disciplinary libraries, such as in history, philosophy, linguistics, or sociology, and don't receive much care or development.

The Roman Catholic Church has always been a minority in Russia, but from 1842 it was able to operate a seminary in St. Petersburg. The extensive library holdings were distributed to other cultural institutions in 1918 when the seminary had to stop its operations. It has been functioning again since 1993 and the library has grown to about 25,000 volumes, half of which is in Russian and the rest in languages such as English, German, French, Italian, Polish, and Latin.

Lutherans, many of non-Russian descent, had an easier plight than Catholics in the Russian Empire and so, at the time of the 1917 Revolution, there were over 3.5 million members. They usually benefited from pastoral training in the Baltics or Germany, and a seminary functioned in St. Petersburg only between 1925 and 1929. Since Perestroika, four small seminaries have been started in Russia. Two are close to St. Petersburg: the library of the seminary of the Evangelical Lutheran Church of Ingria has about 14,000 volumes, and the library in Novo-Saratovka, the successor of the 1925 Lutheran seminary, about 5000–7000 volumes. There are also two seminaries in Siberia, one in Krasnoyarsk and one in Novosibirsk; these two are also responsible for training Lutheran pastors for the Central Asian states (see below). Their libraries are around 5,000 volumes, with books in Russian, German, and English.

In 1988 in Zaoksk, the Adventists were the first non-Orthodox denomination after Perestroika to establish a theological seminary, where they also quickly

Image 1: The library of the St. Petersburg Christian University. © St. Petersburg Christian University

developed an extensive theological library of currently well over 70,000 volumes and just under 10,000 periodicals.

Many theological schools and libraries of other Protestant denominations also came into existence after Perestroika. Some, however, had already successfully operated right after the 1917 Revolution. A flourishing school in St. Petersburg by evangelical Christians and Baptists with minimal library holdings was closed in 1929. Then, in the sixties, the Baptists started a distance education program with no library but reading materials being mailed to students. The beginnings of libraries of Protestant residential theological schools in the early nineties were quite humble, usually just one shelf with whatever theological literature could be scraped together.

Currently, the largest evangelical library is found at the multi-denominational St. Petersburg Christian University (about 28,500 volumes), followed by the Kuban Christian University (about 22,000 volumes), and Moscow Baptist seminary (some 19,000 volumes). There are several other seminaries in Moscow, Bryansk, Omsk, Novosibirsk, Vladivostok. Many of them currently experience significant problems in maintaining their operations after the Russian Ministry of Education's audit in 2018. Several schools, sometimes upon reasoned and often upon implausible allegations, were given high fines and their educational processes were curtailed in different ways. This has increased the atmosphere of fear and unpredictability.

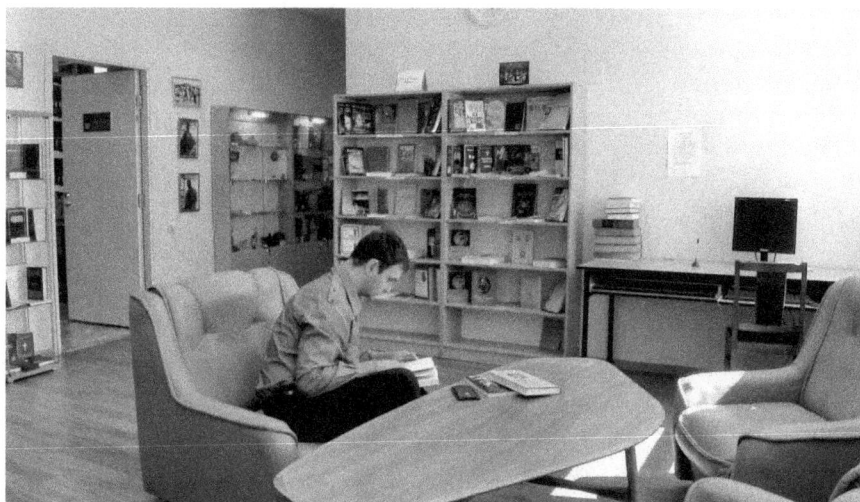

*Image 2: Reading area at the Library of the St. Petersburg Christian University. © St. Petersburg Christian University*

In Belarus, Protestant theological schools are primarily found in the capital Minsk: a Baptist seminary with a library of 12,500 volumes and a Pentecostal seminary; their holdings are around 15,000 volumes.

## *Ukraine*

The history of Orthodox ecclesiastical and theological libraries in Ukraine goes back as far as the 11th century to the Yaroslav library at St. Sophia's Cathedral in Kiev. The Metropolitan Peter Mohyla also greatly contributed to the development of theological schools, book publishing, and ecclesiastical libraries. The library of the Orthodox Kiev Theological Academy, one of the successor schools of the Mohyla Collegium, just before the 1917 communist revolution held around 100,000 volumes and just under 1,000 manuscripts, many of them unique. During communist rule, library holdings came under the jurisdiction of the Vernadsky National Library, and so even today parts of the KTA pre-revolutionary collection are found there. The academy and its library were reopened in 1989 and now serve their own faculty and students with their rich holdings, but also external users.

Image 3: Librarian at the Kiev Orthodox Academy and Seminary consulting future priests.
© Kiev Orthodox Academy and Seminary

As Ukraine always was a spiritually alert area with high numbers of Christians in all denominations, the current scene of theological libraries in Ukraine is much more denominationally diverse.[3] The second-largest religious community, the Ukrainian Greek Catholic church, established formal theological training in 1783. In 1929, the Seminary was transformed into the Greek Catholic Theological Academy. This also marked the beginnings of the library of the Ukrainian Catholic University, its current successor and flagship institution. During the Second World War much of this library was destroyed and so, in 1995, with help from Rome and other places, a new beginning was necessary. The library today holds 146,000 book titles (not all are theological, as the university offers programs in various disciplines), 2,600 periodicals, and several special collections. Besides the University, there are several Greek Catholic theological seminaries, mainly in western Ukraine, with small theological libraries to support priest training. The Roman Catholics have four times fewer members and their own small seminaries with minimal libraries.

Ukrainian Adventists first relied on the Academy in Zaoksk, Russia (see above) for theology training, but then established their own Christian Humanitarian Institute on the outskirts of Kiev with a theological faculty and theology holdings in the library. Master's-level studies are offered in cooperation with Andrews University in the USA. While the total library holdings are around 45,000, the theological collection comes to about 20,000. The other post-Soviet states rely on the Russian and Ukrainian Adventist institutions for training and have no seminaries or libraries of their own.

The Ukrainian Lutherans adhere to two unions: one associated with German Lutherans (they train their pastors in St. Petersburg or Germany) and one Ukrainian. The Ukrainian Lutheran Church had founded a seminary in Ternopil in 1994. It wasn't possible to find information about the seminary library.

After Perestroika, many Protestant and evangelical schools mushroomed in Ukraine. The numbers have gone down somewhat throughout the last years, due to a lack of students and resources. Together with theological schools of the fifteen successor states, evangelical schools founded the Eurasian Accrediting Association (EAAA) in 1992/3, which has the goal to support quality assurance in theological education, foster research and the development of native theology and resources, and provide consultancy. EAAA also invests in library development with highlights such as a librarians' conference in Moscow in 2008, conducted by the author, followed by meetings in 2018 and 2019. A digital library of primarily Russian, Ukrainian, and some English titles was created in 2008–2009 for use by the more than 50 member schools. Individuals–for example, pastors and other church ministers–are also eligible to receive access to the 6,000+ holdings. Due to a common educational and contextual background, the Association is able to strengthen and benefit the usually small to medium-size libraries in different post-Soviet countries. However, legislation in the post-Soviet countries develops in different directions and issues that libraries face locally begin to differ. The language issue and the five years of war between Russia and Ukraine are also affecting relationships and cooperation initiatives (see below).

In the wake of the war, the largest Ukrainian Protestant library at the Donetsk Christian University (with about 40,000 volumes) was destroyed in 2014. Other mid-size theological libraries are found in Kiev (Kiev Theological Seminary, about 31,500 volumes; Evangel Theological Seminary, about 30,000 volumes; Ukrainian Evangelical Theological Seminary, about 25,000 volumes), Odessa (Odessa Theological Seminary, about 23,500 volumes), Kherson (Tavriski Christian Institute, about 26,000 volumes), Lviv (Lviv Theological Seminary, 14,500 volumes), Zaporozhye (Zaporozhye Bible Seminary, 15,000 volumes).

The Ukrainian government so far encourages and fosters education in theology, having already in 2010 created the legal basis for university studies in this discipline up to a doctorate. Many universities offer theology programs, which, however, doesn't mean that sufficient attention is given to the development of library holdings in this area. Programs are added while budgets

Image 4: The library of Divitia Gratiae University. © Universitatea Divitia Gratiae

are cut, university librarians don't have expertise in the subject and literature of theology, and often "old school" librarian thinking prevails (that is, emphasis on custodianship and storage wins out over a focus on service, user needs, new technologies; see Haigh 2009).

## Moldova

Moldova is one of the poorest countries in Europe, riddled by corruption, unstable governments, and very high work emigration. Its population is torn between adherence to Romania (pro-Western wing) and Russia (pro-communist wing), and so educational institutions and libraries, including theological, operate in and combine both languages–Romanian and Russian.

The Orthodox Church trains its clergy at the Academy of Orthodox Theology in Chişinău, started in 1926 and reopened again in 1991. The Academy has an extensive collection, including the archives of the Moldovan Orthodox Church, but it wasn't possible to locate an online catalog of their holdings. The website of the Academy, instead of a link to the catalog, includes links to full-text writings by or about church fathers and saints.

A significant theological library of 24,000 volumes can be found at the Protestant Universitatea Divitia Gratiae. The library is located in a recently constructed building, with expansive study space and great potential for development; its holdings are in Russian, Romanian, and English and can be searched in a Koha-powered OPAC.

## Georgia and Armenia

Both countries are neighbors in the Caucasus region and have some similarities but also clear distinctions. The majority of the population is Orthodox (Armenian Apostolic or Georgian Apostolic respectively), with small minorities of Catholic, Lutheran, and evangelical communities.

The Tbilisi Orthodox Academy was founded in 1988, based on a seminary with a long and difficult history. Today the institution also offers doctoral degrees in Orthodox theology. The library, with holdings of over 5,000 items, has an OpenBiblio OPAC at *http://tsas.ge/bib/opac/index.php*. Several Orthodox and state universities also offer theological studies and have holdings in theology.

Catholics, with a small community of about 10,000 members, after several attempts (see Slantcheva and Levy 2007, 83) were able in 1994 to establish the Sulkhan-Saba Orbeliani Institute of Philosophy, Theology, History, and Culture in Tbilisi, which in 2002 became the Sulkhan-Saba Orbeliani University. Besides humanities and law, it still maintains an ecumenical theology faculty. Its library holdings–mainly in Georgian, Russian, German, and English–come to almost 20,000 items in all disciplines, including theology. The library has an OpenBiblio OPAC at *http://lib.sabauni.edu.ge/opac/index.php* as well as subscriptions to EBSCO and HeinOnline (law).

Protestant training institutions seem to exist more like satellite campuses of theological institutions from other post-Soviet countries. They usually operate in church buildings with very small or no physical libraries. PDF files of titles for required reading are shared or, otherwise, students are directed to purchase their own copies, or else visit the EAAA online library or libraries of local universities.

The Armenian Apostolic Church has operated the Vaskenian Theological Academy since 1990, in close connection with the Gevorkian Theological Seminary. According to the website, the Academy library has approximately 21,000 items in Armenian, English, Russian, and French; no library OPAC was found. The Gevorkian seminary has links to PDFs and audiobooks. Both institutions have close links, including in educational and study resources matters, with Armenian institutions abroad, such as in the USA.

A Baptist seminary has been in existence in Yerevan since the mid-nineties with a library of about 5,000 titles.

## Central Asian "-stan" Countries

Five former Soviet republics–Kyrgyzstan, Kazakhstan, Uzbekistan, Tajikistan, and Turkmenistan–have functioned as independent states now for over 25 years and are similar in their predominantly Islamic context and continuous dependence on other powers in the region, such as Russia, the USA, and various Middle Eastern states. Because Azerbaijan displays many similar aspects in history, Islamic context, and geopolitical power plays, it will also be included in this section even though, geographically, it belongs to the Caucasus region.

While all these countries have a rich cultural and diverse religious heritage, their libraries didn't have much chance to survive for long periods; each successive conquest and, finally, the annexation to the Russian Empire, destroyed or stole the legacy of the previous civilization (Kudryatova 2003). The Russian Empire created libraries for the Russian-speaking population to instill the Orthodox faith and to accelerate the cultural integration of the indigenous population into the Empire.

Christian denominations in all Central Asian states are quite small due to the predominantly Islamic context and restrictive laws that regulate their operations. The Orthodox Church is part of the Russian Orthodox Church and so dependent on the center in Moscow. There are two Orthodox seminaries: in Almaty (founded in 2010) and in Tashkent (founded in 1998), with about 10–15 students each. They also train priests for parishes in other states. No information was found on library holdings, except a list of links on the Almaty seminary site to electronic versions of required reading titles.

The Roman Catholic seminary in Karaganda, Kazakhstan has about 11–12 students and has served all Central Asia since 1998. It was organized with much help from the Vatican and Catholic missionaries from various countries (before that, priest training for Central Asia took place in the Baltic countries or in St. Petersburg). No information on the library was found.

The evangelical denominations, locally called Protestants, are quite diverse; there are large congregations but also house churches, the communities are ethnically mixed or comprise only nationals. Each tradition tends to have its own training institution. Larger theological schools with physical libraries exist in Almaty (Almaty Bible Institute, with a library of about 15,000 volumes) and in

Image 5: The library of the Almaty Bible Institute in Kazakhstan. © Almaty Bible Institute

Bishkek (United Theological Seminary with about 12,000 volumes; Baptist Bible Institute with about 5,000 volumes). Many training initiatives function 'under the radar' as underground seminaries, some are satellite campuses of theological schools from other post-Soviet countries, most use 'less visible' electronic resources instead of a physical library.

Even if a Central Asian theological school provides ministry education, it doesn't go higher than a diploma or bachelor's level; after that, students seek out studies abroad. But even bachelor's studies cannot be sufficiently served with literature in the local language because of low publication and translation output. Theological libraries usually predominantly contain Russian and English holdings with 1–5% native language materials (often translated). They have to carefully watch blacklists of books prohibited by the government so as to not make them available to the public (see Artemyev 2012). The laws on religion and extremism often follow or are similar to Russian laws.

## Library Education

There are no opportunities in post-Soviet countries to receive specific education in theological librarianship. Most of the librarians employed in theological libraries have no professional librarianship education; according to a non-representative survey, in 2017 only about 35% had completed courses for either a library technician degree or a 4-year course for a librarian degree (in state-owned institutions, the number of librarians with professional education is around 60%, see Kouznetsova 2015, 33). The path to librarianship for these persons often includes some way of being connected to a theological school–either as an alumnus/alumna, secretary, academic administrator–and being noticed as having managerial skills, some interest in libraries, and some insight into and understanding of theological literature. Such people are then assigned the duties of running the library, usually in addition to the job they are already doing. Often it is a transitory role because, depending on the direction in which they develop, after some time they may become faculty (pedagogical skills) or academic deans (administrative skills), or move on to completely new areas. If they remain in the field, the question of professional training and development is raised, but it is not easy to solve it while the person is already on the job.

Some have taken courses in librarianship at state universities and were disappointed because of the Soviet ideological leftovers, "old school" library thinking, lack of exposure to new technologies, and because, even though they had received a degree, they still weren't sufficiently prepared for the day-to-day operations of a theological library (Haigh 2009).[4] The Institute of Culture and Arts of the Tomsk State University in Siberia offers a subject, "Orthodox libraries" (Kuzoro 2015), as part of its LIS bachelor's program–a very interesting and useful piece for those who run Orthodox church and seminary libraries. However, it cannot be taken at a distance or online and so remains inaccessible to most of its target group. Read Ministries have supported a two-year program for church librarians in Kremenchug, Ukraine and in Minsk, Belarus, and some theological librarians have graduated from this training. It combines an introduction to the Bible and theology and an introduction to cataloging (Dewey) and other library operations.

State universities and colleges of the post-Soviet states, including programs in librarianship education, are still in the process of many reforms: they transitioned to the Bologna system (three-staged education: bachelor's, master's, doctoral education) around 2003–2005 and have introduced many new initiatives, including competencies-based education and assessment. The first cohort of bachelor's degree holders from the newly designed LIS programs graduated in Russia as recent as 2015, and a few years later in the other successor states

(Klyuev 2015). State universities also offer LIS continuous education programs but, unfortunately, they suffer from financial and personnel shortages and very few can be taken at a distance or online (Kouznetsova 2015, 36).

Much depends, then, on the initiative and enthusiasm of the individual theological librarian to find ways to read up in the discipline,[5] to seek out seminars on relevant topics offered by national libraries (for example, training on cataloging in MARC or authority control), and to follow the work of professional library associations and activities/conferences which they may be offering. The Eurasian Accrediting Association, which comprises primarily evangelical schools, has been running several conferences for librarians' training (EAAA 2019).

## Common Challenges

As mentioned above, 28 years after the break-up of the Soviet Union, its successor states develop in divergent directions but libraries, including theological libraries, still face similar problems due to a common history, a far-too-long transitional period with continuous economic struggles, and a partial return to authoritarian tendencies.

### Scatteredness of Resources

The Bolshevik Revolution in 1917 brought much devastation to libraries of every Christian denomination. Holdings were confiscated and distributed to state libraries and museums or just left to rot. State libraries were not always sure what to do with them: to re-classify and offer them for circulation could cause state sanctions because such holdings were considered dangerous and anti-Soviet; to neglect them would mean to destroy state property. When Stalin in 1943 permitted a re-opening of theological training institutions, Orthodox libraries started to fight for the return of their holdings. At times this was possible, but none were able to regain everything, for various reasons. Many manuscripts and special collections have remained in state libraries. Even if many individual titles were returned to libraries (if they were able to prove ownership before the Revolution!), the coherence and comprehensiveness of the collection were lost. Many reprints of the pre-revolutionary theological scholarship have been produced since the early nineties.

Researchers need to be aware of this history and that materials are haphazardly scattered in various places; much serendipity and fortuitous accidental findings are involved in getting a full overview of a topic. Libraries of theological schools, therefore, usually try to arrange access for their students to the adjacent university and national libraries so as to expand opportunities for access to theological literature. The National Library is expected to hold a copy of each book, including theological books, published in the respective country, even though not all national libraries are equally efficient in this. Many libraries still have closed stacks and smaller libraries especially don't have electronic catalogs that can be accessed through the internet, so often several physical visits to the library become necessary to fully explore the collection.

## Cooperation Initiatives

Even though many ecclesiastical and theological libraries have been started or revived during the last 28 years in the post-Soviet successor countries, there are still limited interconnections between them, inside the same country and across borders, or even inside the same denomination. Cooperation–as, for example, in interlibrary loan, duplicates exchange, document delivery–is often possible only on an informal level, on the basis of personal relationships and trust. This mirrors the state of things in public and university libraries where the old Soviet infrastructures have catastrophically broken down and new lines of cooperation are being established only very slowly. The countries increasingly develop in different directions and Russian as *lingua franca* partly functions for many librarians but also rapidly loses its uniting influence.

Cooperation initiatives usually follow denominational lines and heavily depend on enthusiasts who are able to engage like-minded kindred spirits to invest time and resources into a project. Some small libraries help each other by creating a union catalog. For example, in Minsk, Belarus, five Orthodox libraries, among them the library of the Minsk Orthodox Seminary, run a common catalog (*http://178.124.157.158:8088*). The same seems to be true of the Orthodox library in the Moscow region, which met in March 2019 to discuss various venues for cooperation (Russian Orthodox Church 2019). Greek Catholic libraries in Ukraine are attempting to create a network under the leadership of UCU (the network may or may not go across denominational lines).

The Eurasian Accrediting Association, comprised of about 50 evangelical theological schools, offers support for its member libraries to migrate to the open-source ILS Koha so that they can display their holdings in an OPAC and share bibliographic records through Z39.50. At the same time, the development of a union catalog based on Koha is being discussed. A union catalog of periodicals that member libraries hold is also underway. The EAAA digital library, after ten years of successful operation, needs a thorough overhaul and so plans are underway to migrate to a new platform, expand holdings, and, at the same time, create a D-Space repository with the possibility for member schools to display their theses/dissertations as well as faculty publications. A network of librarians from EAAA schools and, partly, Orthodox seminaries creates venues for

*Image 6: The meeting of Eastern European theological librarians in 2019 in Kiev organized by EEAA. © EEAA*

cooperation with running an annual conference, training sessions for Koha, maintaining a discussion list on social media (Viber and Facebook), and some informal resources exchange.

## Collection Development

There is no real infrastructure to follow theological publications' output, even if one should have a budget to acquire them. Many ecclesiastical publishers, even if they produce serious and useful content, get by without ISBNs, strategic marketing, or effective distribution structures (the latter, however, works only if they are subsidized!). This makes it difficult for libraries to discover and collect such materials. Collection development means following several identified publishers on various social media, maintaining personal contact with the publication house director to find out timely hints, and visiting websites of publishers and internet shops. Periodical publications, difficult to trace in any country and system, add even more challenges.

Collections, especially of Catholic, Lutheran, and Evangelical theological schools, often have large numbers of titles in languages other than the national language, usually English. They are primarily used by faculty because about half to two-thirds of the students do not have sufficient reading and comprehension abilities in English. Publishing cannot supply enough titles in the native language to serve curriculum needs for the different levels of theological training. Librarians need to have at least basic skills in foreign languages to be able to properly catalog the titles or engage in copy cataloging.

## Classification Systems and Cataloging Formats

Collection development and management are complicated by the fact that the existing and widely used classification systems are not useful for theological libraries. The predominant classification system used by state and national libraries and often imprinted on new publications–the Library-Bibliographical Classifications (BBK)–is a leftover from Soviet times (created at the end of the fifties) and therefore ideologically biased in the areas of religion, philosophy, and history. UDC (Universal Decimal Classification) is more often used in technical and medical libraries, and so its Russian version does not provide a sufficiently detailed breakdown for religious and theological materials, plus, having been developed in the West, it displays a bias toward the Western church. The 21$^{st}$ edition of the Dewey Decimal Classification was translated and published in Russian in 2000. This was done by the Russian National Library in order to help librarians navigate OCLC, the Library of Congress, and other libraries in the world. Many theological libraries in post-Soviet countries have adopted it as their classification system. Because the project has been abandoned and no further translations are being made, they are stuck with the 21st edition if they don't know English. Recent DDC editions in English, however, are being produced electronically and require a subscription, which is often unaffordable for libraries. So, libraries sometimes develop their own classification systems or non-standardized, "creative" adaptations of existing ones. This is not conducive for effective search across libraries and also not for cooperative efforts.

Most post-Soviet countries, having been exposed to IFLA's activities after Perestroika, adopted UniMARC as the official cataloging format, with some slight variations in each country (like RusMARC, UkrMARC, BelMARC, etc.). Nevertheless, there are enough leading university and public libraries who–because of software incompatibilities, ignorance, preferences of target libraries in copy cataloging, and possibilities for access to Z39.50 servers–use MARC21(!). Theological librarians, often running their library without professional education, are sometimes not aware of, or are mystified by, the differences in the formats and, accordingly, are confused when copy cataloging doesn't work or when they are told that their bibliographic records don't follow "the standards."

As in theological libraries all over the world, authority control, especially of subject terms/headings, is a recurring issue difficult to solve. The Russian National Library, still leading among the other states, has recently published guidelines for the creation of authority records; these still need to be discussed and approved. There is no infrastructure yet for downloading authority records. And while this would be of great help at least for author records, theological subject terms would need to be created from scratch anyway by theological librarians. So, a multilingual theological thesaurus seems very useful but doesn't yet exist.

## Institutional Issues

Theological libraries receive little prominence in their institutions partly because the focus in education, in state schools but also in denominational institutions, is still mainly on (top-down) lecturing, memorization, and retelling in oral exams rather than on self-directed learning. This can be explained as leftovers from the communist past (where propaganda and education were intertwined and contents were defined centrally and top-down) or as leftovers from modernism (universal truth can be discovered, defined, and taught using directive techniques). Possibly there are also cultural influences with the prevalence in this region of a communal and hierarchical approach rather than a focus on the individual.

The scarce financial base of theological schools in a continuously unpredictable economic context is also a strong reason for library budget cuts. When all departments fight for the money pot, the library is usually disadvantaged because it is not perceived as producing income, because of little advocacy and lobbying from librarians, possibly because of an increasing mentality that libraries offer outdated resources and services and should rather engage in the digitization of required reading titles. The low salaries of theological librarians are concerning, as are the expectation that they combine librarianship with other duties (often secretarial or in academic administration) and the lack of professional education for librarians and lack of strategies for professional development. However, lack of positive change in theological libraries in responding to the current relevant needs of students and faculty will continue to lead to a further disintegration of the libraries' image and perception of usefulness, which will cause another round of library budget cuts.

Because of dissatisfaction with libraries or because users are not aware of library services or are not comfortable with them, faculty and students, like theologians often do, focus on developing their personal print and digital libraries. Each will have collected from the internet, friends, and other sources huge scores of electronic files for educational and ministry purposes, usually in Russian and English.

## Print-Digital Divide and User Training

Theological libraries, not having yet solved the many issues from the past, need to cope with extremely fast developments in technology and to envision effective ways of managing hybrid collections. At the same time, the overwhelming majority of ecclesiastical and theological libraries don't even have an electronic catalog of their holdings and are also rarely featured on the website of the institution. Librarians usually don't have web design skills, and the overworked, often volunteering IT specialist of the institution has no time for this 'less important' component of the school.

The libraries' primary users are millennials who grew up with technology, are affected by globalization, and believe they know all about technology and searching. With their high expectations and an attitude that everything can be found (and, if not, then it needs to be created) in digital form, they are either turned off by libraries or have library anxiety because they don't quite get the specifics of library operations. Students usually arrive with little experience of library use (because public and school libraries are also in poor shape), and so user training and information literacy skills development needs to receive much more attention. However, teaching modes in theological schools (most now give up residential training in favor of distance, online, on-off campus programs) and course assignments don't foster intensive interaction with the library. Librarians are often passive or have no time to creatively reach out to students, design attractive online tutorials, engage in online reference chats, or otherwise help deal with access to quality theological information.

The switch to distance and online education has added challenges for theological libraries to offer digital resources for remote access, so sometimes websites of smaller institutions, instead of references to the physical library and its (non-existent?) OPAC, display a collection of links to PDF copies of key resources. Sometimes the collection and/or creation of electronic resources (for example, in the framework of a learning management system) is found on the job description of the coordinator for distance education and the library is not even included or consulted in the process.

## Conclusion

Theological libraries in post-Soviet countries have gone through the same ups and downs as the seminaries and theological faculties whom they serve. The seventy years of communist and atheist destruction have left their unmistakable legacy that is still felt in subtle and heavy ways. The far-too-long transitional period and continuous economic challenges without much hope for a better future have worn schools and libraries out. Nevertheless, there are many encouraging initiatives, not least in the area of cooperation between libraries, that strive to enable and empower theological librarians to provide the resources and services their parent institutions need in the changing educational process. While many factors need to work together in order to overcome the aforementioned challenges, at the center of change will need to be the librarians themselves who, with a renewed vision and strength, utilize the knowledge and experience of their colleagues worldwide (especially from theological libraries of the majority world), follow and benefit from the developments of librarianship in their own country, and develop new, contextual approaches that respond to the needs in their institutions.

## Notes

1. The Belarusian president Lukashenko once proclaimed himself to be an "Orthodox atheist." For him and for policies in Belarus, this means that religion is instrumentalized for the sake of politics. The Orthodox Church is privileged as part of the cultural heritage, and theological training institutions (of all denominations) are permitted to function as long as they remain inside limits tightly defined by him as president.
2. See, for example, the list of the Justice Department of the Russian Federation at *https://minjust.ru/ru/extremist-materials?field_extremist_content* with about 5,000 titles, as well as the evaluation by Frolov (2012). Writings produced by Jehovah's Witnesses were added to the list recently.
3. According to Elensky (2012), such religious diversity and the lack of a strict link between nation and only one denomination is conducive to a high level of religious tolerance. This made possible less restrictive laws for theological education and libraries.
4. Haigh describes in detail the ideological infiltration of library education before the collapse of the Soviet Union and the attempts of Ukraine to develop a new approach. She also mentions the unpreparedness for library realities after graduation because of how librarianship training is designed and the mismatch between claims and aspirations of university training and what a user then finds in actual daily library processes.

5. The 'Open Science' electronic library at *https://cyberleninka.ru*, other electronic libraries such as *https://rucont.ru/rubric/9*, and larger librarianship journals offer archival and often also current pieces for professional reading.

## Works Cited

Artemyev, A. I. 2012. "Новый закон о религиях в Казахстане: «за» и «против» [The New Law on Religion in Kazakhstan, 'For' and 'Against')." In *Новые вызовы свободе совести в современной России* [*New Challenges for the Freedom of Conscience in Modern Russia*], edited by Ekaterina Elbakyan, 76–82. Moscow: Drevo Zhizni.

EAAA. 2019. "Второй семинар библиотекарей учебных заведений ЕААА." *EAAA. http://www.e-aaa.org/index.php/320-vtoroj-seminar-bibliotekarej-shkol -eaaa*.

Elensky, V. E. 2012. "Религиозная свобода в посткоммунистическом обществе: случай Украины [Religious Freedom in Post-Communist Society: The Case of Ukraine]," in *Новые вызовы свободе совести в современной России* [*New Challenges for the Freedom of Conscience in Modern Russia*], edited by Ekaterina Elbakyan, 69–75. Moscow: Drevo Zhizni.

Frolov, M. A. 2012. "Поиск экстремизма в религиозных текстах: цели и результаты [Searching for Extremism in Religious Texts: Aims and Results]." In *Новые вызовы свободе совести в современной России* [*New Challenges for the Freedom of Conscience in Modern Russia*], edited by Ekaterina Elbakyan, 93–97. Moscow: Drevo Zhizni.

Haigh, Maria. 2009. "Two Steps Forward, One Step Back: Ideological and Historical Aspects of Library and Information Science Education in Independent Ukraine." In *Advances in Library Administration and Organization*, vol. 27, edited by W. Graves, J. Nyce, J. Golden, and D. Williams, 1–24. Bingley: Emerald Group Publishing. *https://doi.org/10.1108/S0732– 0671(2009)0000027006*.

Klyuev, V. K. 2015. "Новые реалии и перспективы высшего библиотечно-информационного образования [New Realities and Prospects of the Higher Library and Information Education]." *Вестник Томского государственного университета. Культурология и искусствоведение* [*Herald of the Tomsk State University, Culture and Arts*] 1, no. 17: 79–85. *http://www.doi.org/10 .17223/22220836/17/12*.

Kouznetsova, Tatiana Y. 2015. "Повышение квалификации и переподготовка –базовое звено непрерывного библиотечно-информационного образования [Training and Retraining–Basic Element of Continuous LIS Education]." *Труды Санкт-Петербургского государственного института культуры и искусств* [*Works of the St. Petersburg State Institute of Culture and Arts*] 205: 32–37.

Kudryatova, D. K. 2003. "Развитие библиотек Узбекистана и их роль в жизни Республики [Development of Uzbek Libraries and Their Role in the Life of the Republic]." In *Библиотеки национальных академий наук: проблемы функционирования, тенденции развития* [*Libraries of National Academies of Sciences: Operational Problems, Tendencies of Development*], 302–313. *http://dspace.nbuv.gov.ua/handle/123456789/34216*.

Kuzoro, Kristina A. 2015. "Учебный курс «Православные библиотеки» в системе подготовки специалистов библиотечно-информационной сферы [Academic Course 'Orthodox Libraries' in the Education of Specialists in the Library Sphere]." *Вестник Томского государственного университета. Культурология и искусствоведение* [*Herald of the Tomsk State University, Culture and Arts*] 1, no. 17: 90–94. *http://www.doi.org/10.17223/22220836/17/14*.

Russian Orthodox Church. 2019. "Состоялась встреча руководителей и представителей библиотек православных учебных заведений Москвы и Московской области." *Patriarchia.ru*. *http://www.patriarchia.ru/db/text/5398077.html*.

Slantcheva, Snejana and Daniel C. Levy, eds. 2007. *Private Higher Education in Post-Communist Europe: In Search of Legitimacy*. New York: Palgrave.

# CHAPTER 7

# Theological Libraries in Latin America

ÁLVARO PÉREZ

## Introduction

In 1492, Christianity arrived with the Spaniards to the New World, which would be known as the American continent, where it clashed with the existing religions and, shortly afterward, it was imposed on the newly discovered continent. A religious acculturation process was begun. The ways of the Old World were implanted on the new, such as in mission work, theological training, and libraries. Christianity had already evolved into various forms in Europe, and as colonial European powers began arriving, so did these other forms. Initially, they can be divided into two main categories: Catholicism and, later, Protestantism.

## Religion and Books in the Pre-Hispanic Period and the Conquest

Of an important number of civilizations and peoples on the American continent, three stand out: the Maya, the Aztec, and the Inca. The Mayan culture became the most advanced civilization in America. The pre-Columbian cultures also had their religious systems (Conrad and Demarest 1984; Batalla Rosado and Luis de Rojas 2008; Sohen Suarez and George 2011, 123–47). Religion was very relevant in the Mayan world (Rivera Dorado 2006). Its most important known literary text is the Popol Vuh ("Book of the Council," or "Book of the Community"). It consists of mythical-historical accounts of a pre-Hispanic Mayan group (De la Garza Camino and Coronado 2002, 29) and explains the existence of the Mayan world (Christenson 2003). Because of their quest for knowledge, the Mayans had an important bibliographical production (codices) that amounted to libraries.

On October 12, 1492, three Spanish ships landed on a Caribbean island. It was not the first incursion from other lands, but this one had the intention of settling permanently in this new world, and it was determined to conquer it and subdue it. Once settled in the Caribbean, the *conquistadores* embarked on expeditionary trips through the mainland. On April 21, 1519, they reached the coast of present-day Mexico and, on November 8 of that year, a meeting between the Spanish leader and the Aztec emperor took place. The *conquistadores* attacked and captured the Aztec capital on August 13, 1521. In 1532, the Incan empire was also brought to an end. It was the last of the great civilizations of the American continent. It was the end of Pre-Hispanic America and the beginning of European-colonized America.

It was important for the church to have religious leaders to spread the Gospel, but also people to look after the interests of the Spanish Crown in its colonies. After the conquest, the Spanish friars arrived in a larger number with the goal of imposing a new religion–the Iberian world's version of Christianity–and, as much as possible, to eradicate the previous ones. The religious orders were dedicated to the task of introducing the Native Americans to Christian culture (Latourette 1970, 105). In this process, education played a relevant role (Deiros 1992, 287). The Church's reality in America was somehow similar to the one in Europe during the Middle Ages, when monasteries and abbeys were the only centers of knowledge. Because of this, priests and monks could exert great influence on the population. The colonial education pursued established goals from its onset (Deiros 1992, 368). There was the need to minister spiritually to Spanish immigrants and their descendants. This was the task of the secular clergy who built temples, organized the ecclesiastical structure according to the Spanish model with parishes and episcopal seats, and set up seminaries for the preparation of priests. The Inquisition helped to keep the Roman Catholic faith of the peninsula free from contamination (Deiros 1992, 274). Where books already existed in the indigenous cultures of Mexico and Central America, "they were seized and destroyed as an inadmissible obstacle to the effective imposition of the invader's ideology" (Hallewell 1995, 38). To Diego de Landa (1524–1579) and other Franciscan friars, the Mayan writings were the result of diabolical practices and, as he (1966, 105) states:

> We found a large number of books in these characters and, as they
> contained nothing in which were not to be seen as superstition and lies of

*the devil, we burned them all, which they [the Maya] regretted to an amazing degree, and which caused them much affliction.*

On July 12, 1562, in an *auto de fe* ("act of faith"),[1] De Landa, who served as the local Franciscan provincial, along with other things, burned the codices. After the Spaniards, other European colonial powers–Holland, Portugal, England, France– also found their way to America, bringing with them their versions of Christianity.

Outside of some civil universities, education in Latin America during the colonial period was entirely in the hands of the Roman Catholic Church. Religious orders played an important role in its development. The first school in America was established in Santo Domingo in 1505. In Mexico, the Native Americans and mestizos (persons of mixed ancestry) who lived far from the populated centers received almost no schooling. Secondary education did not serve general cultural purposes, nor did it provide the students with the necessary practical knowledge. Its orientation was markedly philosophical and theological. It did not have a popular character and was rather intended for the upper classes. It was driven by the clergy, first by the Dominicans and later especially by the Jesuits, or by civil servants of the colony after the expulsion of the Jesuits (Deiros 1992, 369).

## The Beginnings of the Christian Library in America

The Western library came to America together with religion. The *conquistadores*, after taking political control of Mexico and Peru–the two most developed civilizations at that time–proceeded to consolidate their power through proselytizing their sovereign's new subjects. The book was one of the ways to serve this purpose. In 1533, the Emperor ordered and provided money to finish the printing of twelve thousand booklets that were to be sent to New Spain for the instruction of the natives (Griffin 2015, 255). Initially, literary production was mainly confined to materials written by missionaries for catechetical work. These were commissioned from Spanish printers. The Crombergers of Seville were one of the selected printers. They were particularly interested in America both as an export market for their books and as a place for direct investment in other fields (Hallewell 1995, 38). The Emperor gave John Cromberger a monopoly both on printing in New Spain and on the export of prints there. According to this real provision they were required to send to Mexico the "books of all faculties and doctrines" that were needed in the colony and, in return, nobody but them could export these books or *cartillas* (Griffin 2015, 256). In 1539, the Crombergers sent a printer to Mexico City–the first New World publishing house–and, a quarter of a century later, another to Lima, Peru (Halewell 1995, 38–9). In the next century, other American cities also had printers. The Crombergers published many of the most frequently circulated titles in the Indies: liturgical editions, books of hours, devotional works, the writings of the Church Fathers in Spanish (Griffin 2015, 268). First, the books arrived in small quantities and then, later, were transformed into libraries. During the sixteenth and seventeenth centuries, commercial fleets transported large quantities of books–hundreds and thousands of volumes–from the Old World to the New. This is how many of the books that circulated in Spain were also found in the Indies, the latter being a smaller market (Dill and Knauer 1993, 37). But in the Spanish Empire, this was not a free market. In colonial times, censorship was strictly enforced. This was practiced both in Europe and on the American continent. In 1559, the Catholic Church published the *Index librorum prohibitorum* ("List of Prohibited Books"), which banned 550 authors and proscribed some individual titles. The Inquisition controlled the enforcement of these norms through the *Index* itself, visits to bookstores and libraries both public and private, border surveillance, visits to ships arriving at their ports, and the obligation of the inhabitants to denounce the illegal possession of these works. The books could also be printed in selected indigenous languages (Griffin 2015, 255).

In many cases, the missionaries who left for America brought with them books, either bought or from their convents (Griffin 2015, 259), that contributed to the libraries formed inside the colonial convents, both as support for the study of the religious and for their pastoral work. The Catholic Church's missionary orders were most notable for book collecting, particularly the Dominicans and Franciscans, who were part of the very first expeditions. The Church was also responsible for staffing and running the universities in Mexico City, Lima, and Santo Domingo. All were decreed in 1551, the first on the continent (Hallewell, 1995, 39). It was the friars who initiated a very simple form of librarianship in this hemisphere, put into practice from colonial times. The most famous of all were the Jesuits, who began to work in the Americas only ten years after the foundation of their order. They settled in Brazil, Paraguay, and Argentina. Over time, the Jesuits became the largest missionary order in Brazil and were pioneers in many works. They arrived in Mexico in 1572, when the Church was already fully constituted (Deiros 1992, 288). The Jesuits became the most influential of the orders. Their members were more inclined to the natural and human sciences (O'Malley, Bailey, Harris, and Kennedy 1999), to history and modern philosophy, than to theology itself (O'Malley 2014). They were committed to cultural conquest and educational activities. As libraries grew, the Jesuits established traditions of librarianship that were more developed in Brazil than in any other European colony (Grover 1993, 267). The expelling of the Jesuits from Brazil in 1759 and from Spanish America in 1767 resulted in the dispersion of some of the finest libraries then existing in the Western Hemisphere. It was an unmitigated cultural disaster. The Jesuit colleges were taken over by other religious orders that, with time, transformed into Latin American universities (Hallewell 1995, 39).

## Christian Evolution in the Old World and Its Impact on the New

After its arrival in America, Christianity continued to evolve in both worlds. In Iberian America, the peninsular version was imposed, but the predominance of the Catholic Church in Western Europe was shaken by the crisis of the 16th century and the rise of the Protestant Reformation. Through migration and trade, Protestantism found its way into the New World. As time went by, it increased its presence in Spanish America, where practitioners' spiritual needs had to be taken care of. This was done by Protestant European churches that sent missionaries to serve their small communities (Míguez Bonino 1997, 3). The evangelization work on this part of the continent had been underway for quite some time. Dr. James Thompson had arrived in Buenos Aires in 1818, although his work was mainly with the British and Foreign Bible Society and it was not directed to the establishment of any church. In 1836, the Rev. J. Dempster, to whom the Methodist work owes its origin, arrived in this same city. Protestant Christian movements were attracted to the idea of missionary work to convert the non-Christian world to their religious views. Missionary societies were established for this purpose. Catholicism in Spanish America remained unchanged and opposed to versions of Christianity other than its own. From the mid–19th century, an important shift took place, and United States Protestantism emerged as the main source of missionary drive in Latin America. From then on, a movement was born to counteract this position. In New York, in 1913, the Committee on Cooperation in Latin America (CCLA) was established. In 1916, the CCLA held the *Congress on Christian Work in Latin America* in the city of Panama. Two other congresses were also held: Montevideo (1925) and Havana (1929), to deal with evangelization in Latin America. These congresses also followed the ecumenical trend for the future to come.

In the American continent, the evangelical church developed its diversity, largely influenced by United States Protestantism. In the course of a considerable period, there was an evolution that contributed to the emergence of several religious thoughts, such as fundamentalism, conservatism, and evangelicalism (Harris 1998), not necessarily understood in the same way outside the US. Pentecostalism would also be an important religious movement. It became a fast-growing movement within the Protestant Latin American church. Among the evangelicals, the fundamentalist movement arose in the 1920s against modernist or liberal theology in the mainline Protestant churches of the United States, and over time they established their churches (Galindo 1992; Marsden 2006). Through missionary outreach, this thought and others also spread to other regions. In the United States, a movement had been brewing whose influence would transcend that country. The National Association of Evangelicals (NAE) was formed in 1942, becoming a relevant evangelical organization (Carpenter 1997). In the following years, NAE and its associated groups would become a powerful and influential force for those who embraced evangelicalism. Between 1962 and 1965, the Second Vatican Council took place. Its ecumenical spirit eased tensions between Catholicism and other Christian churches, and certainly for the Latin American churches. Latin American Protestantism has been greatly influenced by United States Protestantism–fundamentalist and conservative–and ecumenical views, the latter as a legacy of the *Edinburgh Missionary Conference* and CCLA congresses. In 1966, the Billy Graham Association financed the First Latin American Congress of Evangelization called CLADE (*Congreso Latinoamericano de Evangelización*), "Action in Christ for a Continent in Crisis," November 21-30, 1969, in Bogotá, Colombia (Zaldivar 2006, 93). In 1970 in Cochabamba, Bolivia, the Latin American Theological Fraternity (FTL) was constituted. Other CLADEs, the conservative line of Protestantism (see Prien 1985; Bastian 1990; Deiros 1992), would be held in the years to come, and these were sponsored by the Latin American Theological Fraternity (FTL). In November 1982, the *Consejo Latinoamericano de Iglesias* (Latin American Council of Churches) was established to promote unity among Christians on the continent. The effervescent movement that took place in the region in the 1960s would become relevant to the church and eventually lead to the emergence of Latin American theology. These influences would permeate theological education in the region.

The evangelization drive that was undertaken mainly from the United States to Latin America required a massive missionary workforce. Several mission societies were established according to denominational interests, which were responsible for raising funds for their missionary endeavors. As work progressed, elementary and secondary schools were established alongside congregations. But also, denominational seminaries were established, usually following closely the educational philosophy and curriculum of conservative evangelical seminaries of the North Atlantic churches that supported these communities (George 2007, 15). But evangelization continued to be a priority. To this end, ways were constantly sought to improve its efficiency. On-site theological training was one of these ways. The theory was revised and improved by practice. Ideally and briefly stated: under missionary guidance–the "true faith"–native workers, mainly young, would be trained in a Bible school and then sent to the mission fields to do evangelistic work (preaching and church planting), hopefully with a multiplier effect. Eventually, Bible schools would transform into Bible institutes, seminaries, and colleges. Arriving from the North–the United States and Canada–the missionary workforce was English-speaking, a challenge in the mainly Spanish-speaking region and because there was also a Portuguese-speaking territory. Partly because of the cultural influence in their countries of origin and because of the need to do their work, the missionaries acquired books for their personal libraries. Most of them were in English, some in Spanish, and a few in other languages, depending on the missionary's immigrant background. These collections developed around the owners' subject areas of interest. In the beginning, there were no publishing houses for Protestant religious materials in Spanish. Initially, the production of books in this language was done through the existing publishing houses for the Anglo-Saxon world. The American Tract Society (established in 1825) is the continuation of previous initiatives: the New York Tract Society of 1812, the New England Tract Society of 1814, and the Religious Tract Society of London, which began in 1799. These may be the first books to meet academic information needs, which would later become the basis for institutional libraries. For a few more decades the English-speaking staff would still be predominant, and so would the English-language literature for the missionary. Initially, literature was produced in English and, as the need arose, it was translated into Spanish. With time, publishing houses for this type of book would emerge in Latin America, such as La Casa Unida de Publicaciones, S. A., La Aurora Publishing House, and Editorial Caribe. The latter began in Costa Rica in 1949 under the auspices of the Latin American Mission.

As an outcome of the Edinburgh Missionary Conference, the International Missionary Council (IMC) was created in 1921. During the 1957/1958 IMC Assembly in Ghana, an important monetary contribution was reported. Mr. John Rockefeller, Jr. had donated $2,000,000 for the establishment of a Theological Education Fund (hereafter called the TEF). The earliest date when the operations were to begin was July 1, 1958. This fund aimed at the advancement of theological education in Asia, Africa, and Latin America–regions that were emerging from colonialism. Essentially, its goal was to improve the level of scholarship at the institutions (Ecumenical Theological Education 2008). James F. Hopewell (1929–1984) became first the associate director (1960–1964) and then the director (1964–1970) of the TEF. In this position, he traveled throughout Latin America, Africa, and Asia, visiting theological faculties (Lienemann-Perrin 1981). In the early 1960s, an initiative was conceived that would contribute significantly to the cause of theological libraries. The librarian Raymond Philip Morris (1904–1990) would be instrumental in this matter. In 1958, TEF asked Morris to survey theological library needs. In 1959, he spent four months in Southeast Asia. During this time, he observed that the libraries he visited often lacked trained personnel and that the North American books on which they depended had little to do with the work of theological education. Morris collaborated with an international team of scholars to compile a classified bibliography of nearly 6000 titles, the *Theological Book List*—a project that would support seminars in Africa, Asia, Latin America, and the Southeast Pacific. The eligible schools were able to select books from the list to include in their collections (Davis 2003). In Latin America, several libraries benefited from this program.

In the conservative line, and with logistical support from the Billy Graham Evangelistic Association, CONELA (Latin American Evangelical Confraternity) was founded in 1982. In the line of ecumenism, the Latin American and Caribbean Ecumenical Theological Education Community (CETELA) was created in 1988. The Latin American theological associations include, among others, the following: ASIT (Association of Seminaries and Theological Institutions—in the Southern Cone); ASTE (Association of Evangelical Theological Seminaries—in Brazil); AETAL (Evangelical Association of Theological Education of Latin America—in Brazil); ALIET (Latin American Association of Institutions of Theological Education—in Central America and Mexico). Besides coordinating and developing theological education programs throughout the region, later these associations would also be concerned about theological library improvement.

Missionary staff came from a cultural background with a deep-rooted library culture. During their seminary training back home, mainly the United States, they had been exposed to library life and, most likely, had been able to "take a closer look" at this resource–that books are somehow organized in the shelves, that they can be accessed by information recorded on catalog cards, and also that books can be checked out by a simple system. This was the case in the United States, where librarianship had already reached a developed stage. Latin American library schools would appear almost four decades later, first in Argentina (1922), then in Panama (1941), Brazil (1942), and so on until reaching the rest of the Latin American region.

Julia Pettee (1872–1967), the librarian at Union Theological Seminary in New York City, devised a classification system that would be known as Union Classification (Pettee 1967). It took her several years to put it together, and finally it was published in 1939. At one point, the Pettee System was adopted by a significant number of North American theological libraries. The Latin American theological institutions had small incipient library collections, a few larger than others, reasonably managed. As a surcharge on his/her functions, a missionary could assume the management of the seminary's library. This staff member would implement faculty agreements on library matters, working alongside (in those cases where one existed) a library committee. In general, he–or she–would be in charge of policies, acquisitions, schedule, basic services, and, when stipulated, with students as his–or her–assistants.

Eventually, news about the Union Classification system, specifically developed for theological libraries, spread to the region. It was also the choice for a good number of other libraries in different parts of the world, including several in Latin America. On the missionary-librarian desk some suitable texts could be found, such as *Aker's Simple Library Cataloging* (Akers 1977), an edition of the *ALA Rules for Filing Catalog Cards* (ALA 1942), and *A Theological Library Manual* (Newhall 1970). As to Union Classification, it was used for some time. Two valuable features of a tool are its universality and currentness. If there is no entity to update it for its entire user community, then isolated updates will produce uneven results. In Latin America, the libraries opted mostly for the Dewey Decimal Classification system.

## The Latin American Approach

In Latin America, the transition from an artisanal to a professional library education began in Sâo Paulo, Brazil in 1929, although there is evidence that it had begun earlier in other regions: in Mexico, first in 1912 and later in 1922; in Rio de Janeiro in 1914. In 1920, the American Library Association launched its Latin American program by adopting a broad policy on library issues with other countries. The Committee for Library Cooperation with Latin America operated as a means of exchange of information, consultation, and assistance between libraries in the United States and Canada, on the one hand, and in Latin American countries, on the other (Gropp 1948). In the libraries of biblical institutes and seminaries, it is a different story. In these, the missionary way still prevails. A library would be fortunate if visited by a professional theological librarian from the North. Each one attends to its own needs and there are no contacts with others or with the already developing Latin American librarianship, and it will be so for some decades to come.

Two resources were developed to support theological research in Latin America: *Bibliografia Teológica Comentada* (1973–1990) was edited and published by the Instituto Superior de Estudios Teológicos[2] in Buenos Aires, Argentina, and *Bibliografia Bíblica Latino-Americana,* published by the Programa Ecuménica de Pós-Graduagao en Ciencias da Religiáo of Sáo Bernardo do Campo in Sáo Paulo, Brazil–an eight-volume project that sought to collect information on biblical publications between 1988 and 1995. At that time, it was a very time-consuming task, not to mention the required financial resources.

Image 1: Library of the Latin American Biblical University in San José, Costa Rica. © Álvaro Pérez

## LIS Education

In Latin America the secular wave of training took place in the 1940s, leading to the subsequent establishment of library schools. The theological schools' associations have been one of the most successful experiments in evangelical collaboration, bringing together a broad spectrum of Latin American evangelical institutions in interesting projects. Once the theological schools became affiliated to their respective association–ASIT, ASTE, AETAL, ALIET–either by region and/or affinity of thought, there were some issues about which to be concerned, such as accreditation, exchange of professors and students, academic resource sharing, and library improvement. Theological librarianship training took place in the 1980s and early 1990s when conditions were met for this stage, such as the increase in the number of theological institutions and the rise in their formation level, which demanded more library support. Some of the staff who worked in these libraries did not have enough training, or had none at all. Library education followed the traditional way, learning by practice from day to day. Therefore, the schools aimed either for better trained clerics or, if affordable, professional librarians. The Latin American theological associations organized workshops to train library staff. ALIET organized regional theological library workshops: 1983, in San José, Costa Rica; 1990, in Guatemala City, Guatemala; 1991, again in Guatemala City; 1993, in Mexico City, Mexico. In 1997, ALIET, CETELA, and RLIT (*Red Latinoamericana de Información Teológica*, known in English as LATIN) held a similar event in Quito, Ecuador. One more took place also in 2000 in Quito, under the auspices of CETELA and RLIT. These workshops were technically oriented. Something similar was experienced in the Southern Cone, where library concerns were approached by ASIT. An entire issue of *Encuentro y Diálogo* (no. 10, 1994), ASIT's journal, was dedicated to the subject of libraries and their work, with the following contents: "What is the function of the theological library?" "The library: its functions," "The theological library in the perspective of the student," "The library and the curriculum," "Libraries and their needs," "The librarian/teaching team in user/student training," "The journals that aren't and would be so necessary," and "The pastoral library." On the other hand, Latin American theological education continued to evolve. At the end of the millennium, a survey of international theological colleges was conducted. It provided some interesting data for Latin America. With respect to degrees, the theological institutions were offering: certificate, 10.45%; diploma, 15.68%; bachelor's, 38.56%, licentiate, 13.72%; master's, 14.37%; and doctorate, 7.18% (Gilmore 1997).

While the above was taking place, some library staff had managed to get librarianship degrees, and at least three of them had become affiliated to Atla (established in the US in 1946 as the American Theological Library Association). A professional librarian meant a better-managed library, which can offer a greater range of need-based information services. This was an important shift that greatly enhanced the library view, way beyond the technical one. *Aker's Library Cataloging*, Newhall's *Manual*, handwritten and typed notes for doing library work were eventually replaced with professional tools, along with a new library vision. By then, more institutions were hiring professional librarians.

## Latin American Theological Library Association (RLIT)

An effort was made to seek better ways to improve library work using a collaborative approach. In the later part of 1993, an attempt was made to contact theological libraries in the Latin American region. After succeeding, a call was made to meet in 1996 in San José, Costa Rica, to discuss the possibilities of establishing a Latin American Theological Library Association (*Red*

Image 2: Attendees at the 2<sup>nd</sup> Meeting of RLIT in La Paz, Bolivia, 1998. © Álvaro Pérez

*Latinoamericana de Información Teológica*–RLIT). This new organization met every two years in a different Latin America country (La Paz, Bolivia; Quito, Ecuador; Havana, Cuba; Mexico City; Buenos Aires, Argentina; Asunción, Paraguay). During these theological librarianship congresses numerous subjects were approached, such as: Latin American theological librarianship, Latin American theological development, Latin American theological professional needs, Latin American theological librarianship trends, theology and theological education, the theological library user, theological information services in Latin America, new information technologies, reference works in theological libraries, and practical experiences with library automation.

Besides presentations, also workshops, library visits, and library products exhibits were scheduled. The RLIT congresses were held until 2008, with the last one taking place in Asunción, Paraguay. A newsletter, *Boletín del Bibliotecario Teológico Latinoamericano* [*Latin American Theological Librarian Newsletter*] was edited as a means of information for the theological library community. A theological library manual–*Formación y organización de una biblioteca teológica: Un manual para la capacitación* [Creation and Organization of a Theological Library: A Training Manual] (Pérez and Laureano 2000)–was edited for non-professional librarians. Libraries already had access to existing universal classification systems and to the *Anglo-American Cataloguing Rules,* 2nd edition (AACR2), Spanish translation. Some libraries had an earlier version. An

*Introduction to Theological Libraries*

indexation tool specifically for theological libraries had to be created since there was none. There was a subject headings list and thesaurus for public and college libraries. This is how the "Subject headings list for theology" (Duarte and Rodríguez 1998) came into being.

The *Catálogo colectivo de publicaciones periódicas* [Collective catalogue of periodical publications] was edited by Brazilian theological librarians as a tool that aimed at research work (*Catálogo colectivo* 1999). Also, a "Latin American directory of theological libraries and librarians" (Pérez and Rivoir 2000) was edited. The idea was to have information on available resources in the region, both libraries and librarians. It was expected that RLIT would consolidate and, through collective work, could be able to produce a set of resources–a few of them already underway–to serve the purposes of the network.

## Conclusion

As this is written, Latin American theological institutions face several challenges: society's shift to secularism, lower student enrollment, financial constraints, and those that have facilities of a certain size have problems in maintaining them. There is still a great degree of dependence on overseas funding, but reality has changed. Traditional church-related funding organizations are experiencing reduced financial income, which in turn means less money to be allocated to church-related ministries in some developing regions, where other pressing needs are being taken into account. Within the institutions themselves, and when financial resources are scarce, priorities would also be taken into account; whatever is available will be allocated accordingly, and libraries do not often appear to be among them. Teaching staff and students are priorities–the *raison d'être* of the institution. In Latin America, theological education is mostly related to a ministry, a special call, from which no profit is expected. Because of this, financial assistance must be provided to students. Despite the above–and within the described tight situation–theological schools continue to offer theological training, with the implied limitations. The advent of improved and financially more affordable ICTs has enabled them to set up virtual platforms for their educational programs, incorporating along with required library services. These services aim to meet the needs of the academic programs being offered, and these do not necessarily support research beyond this level. However, some institutions engage in research and publishing activities. In this part of the world, a tight budget means very little money. Collection development–for books, journals, reference works, and other resources, either physical or digital–remains a major pressing need, as new material is constantly published. There is also the need to reduce the risk of resorting to a bibliography with some degree of obsolescence. Desirably, collection updating should be mainly done in Spanish and Portuguese, the major languages of the region, although there are also some widely used indigenous languages. Some may think that, in the Internet Age, theological information is freely available, making it unnecessary to invest so much in libraries and librarians. While this part may be true, it is a limited solution. Users–who can afford or access information technology–may choose to download information from legal and illegal sites, enabling them to develop digital personal collections. Access to commercial databases such as EBSCO and ProQuest is not a possibility. Open access repositories have been welcomed but are still distant from the sophistication of well-known commercial databases. Although it must be conceded that, over time, they have increased both in number and quality. The theological library landscape has gone through major changes in the last decades. Besides the aforementioned challenges, there are a few others to be concerned about, such as better-staffed libraries (hopefully with trained librarians), improved ICT access and equipment renovation, adequate departmental infrastructure, and better-designed and implemented information services. The old belief that library work is related to technical matters and custodial functions is still to be overcome. Sadly, RLIT faded away with a change of leadership. In can be said that Latin American theological librarianship returned to its isolated ways in a world that has changed. Something must be done in order to collectively approach its current challenges.

## Notes

1. A public act organized by the tribunal of the Holy Inquisition in which the condemned abjured their sins, repenting and thus achieving their reconciliation with the Catholic Church. The public performance of the act was to serve as a lesson to all the faithful gathered in the public square or place selected for this purpose.
2. An outstanding institution, with the largest theological library in Latin America, it was closed in 2015. At the time of this writing, the future of its library is unknown.

# Works Cited

Akers, Susan Grey. 1977. *Aker's Simple Library Cataloging.* 6th edition. Metuchen, NJ: Scarecrow. There is a Spanish translation: *Catalogación sencilla para bibliotecas.* 1983. Pax-México: Librería Carlos Césarman.

American Library Association. 1942. *ALA Rules for Filing Catalog Cards.* Chicago, IL: American Library Association.

Bastian, Jean-Pierre. 1990. *Historia del protestantismo en América Latina.* México: CUPSA.

Batalla Rosado, Juan José and José Luis de Rojas. 2008. *La religión azteca.* Madrid: Trotta.

Carpenter, Joel A. 1997. *Revive Us Again: The Reawakening of American Fundamentalism.* New York: Oxford University Press.

Catálogo colectivo de publicaciones periódicas. 1999. São Leopoldo, Brasil: Rede Latinoamericana de Informação Teológica, com o apoio da Escola Superior de Teología.

Christenson, Allen J., trans. 2003. *Popol Vuh: Sacred Book of the Quiché Maya People.* Mesoweb. *http://www.mesoweb.com/publications/Christenson /PopolVuh.pdf.*

Cohen Suarez, Ananda and Jeremy James George. 2011. *Handbook to Life in the Inca World.* New York: Facts On File.

Conrad, Geoffrey W. and Arthur A. Demarest. 1984. *Religion and Empire: The Dynamics of Aztec and Inca Expansionism.* Cambridge: Cambridge University Press.

Davis, Donald G., Jr., ed. 2003. *Dictionary of American Library Biography.* Second supplement. Westport, CT: Libraries Unlimited.

Deiros, Pablo Alberto. 1992. *Historia del cristianismo en América Latina.* Buenos Aires: Fraternidad Teologica Latinoamericana.

De la Garza Camino, Mercedes and Martha Ilia Nájera Coronado, eds. 2002. *Religión maya.* Madrid: Trotta.

De Landa, Diego. 1966. *Relaciones de las cosas de Yucatán.* Ninth edition. México: Editorial Porrúa. There is an English translation: William Gates, trans. 1937. *Yucatan Before and After the Conquest.* Baltimore: The Maya Society.

Dill, Hans-Otto and Gabriele Knauer, eds. 1993. *Diálogo y conflicto de culturas: estudios comparativos de procesos transculturales entre Europa y América Latina.* Frankfurt am Main: Vervuert.

Duarte, Giselle and Margoth Rodríguez. 1998. *Lista de encabezamientos de materia para teología.* Dir. Álvaro Pérez. San José: Red Latinoamericana de Información Teológica.

Ecumenical Theological Education. "The Establishment of the Theological
Education Fund (TEF) During the IMC Assembly in Ghana, 1957/1958." 2008.
*Ministerial Formation* 110 (April): 12–14.

Galindo, Florencio. 1992. *El Protestantismo fundamentalista. Una experiencia
ambigua para América Latina.* Estella, Navarra: Verbo Divino.

George, Sherron Kay. 2007. "Ecumenical Theological Education in Latin America,
1916–2005." *International Bulletin of Missionary Research* 31, no. 1 (January).

Gilmore, Alec, ed. 1997. *International Directory of Theological Colleges.* Geneva:
WCC Publications.

Griffin, Clive. "Los Cromberger y los impresos enviados a las colonias españolas
en América durante la primera mitad del siglo XVI, con una coda filipina [The
Crombergers and Printed Books Sent to the Spanish Colonies in the Americas
in the First Half of the Sixteenth Century, with a Philippine coda]." *Titivillus* 1
(2015).

Gropp, Arthur E. 1948. "Education for Librarianship in the Americas." *The Library
Quarterly: Information, Community, Policy* 18, no. 2 (1948): 108–117.

Grover, Mark L. 1993. "The Book and the Conquest: Jesuit Libraries in Colonial
Brazil." *Libraries & Culture* 28, no. 3 (Summer).

Hallewell, Laurence. 1995. "Rare Books in Latin American Libraries." *IFLA Journal*
21, no. 1.

Harris, Harriet A. 1998. *Fundamentalism and Evangelicals.* Oxford: Oxford
University Press.

Latourette, Kenneth S. 1970. *A History of the Expansion of Christianity,* vol. 3,
*Three Centuries of Advance.* Grand Rapids: Zondervan.

Lienemann-Perrin, Christine. 1981. *Training for a Relevant Ministry: A Study of
the Contribution of the Theological Education Fund.* Madras: Christian
Literature Society, in association with the Programme on Theological
Education of the World Council of Churches, Geneva, Switzerland.

Marsden, George M. 2006. *Fundamentalism and American Culture.* New York:
Oxford University Press.

Míguez Bonino, José. 1997. *Faces of Latin American Protestantism: 1993 Carnahan
Lectures.* Grand Rapids, MI: W. B. Eerdmans Pub. Co.

Newhall, Jannette E. 1970. *A Theological Library Manual.* London: Theological
Education Fund.

O'Malley, John W. 2014. *The Jesuits: A History from Ignatius to the Present.*
Lanham, Maryland: Rowman and Littlefield.

———, Gauvin Alexander Bailey, Steven J. Harris, and T. Frank Kennedy, eds. 1999.
*The Jesuits: Cultures, Sciences, and the Arts, 1540–1773.* Toronto: University of
Toronto Press.

*Introduction to Theological Libraries*

Pettee, Julia. 1967. *Classification of the Library of Union Theological Seminary in the City of New York*. New York, Union Theological Seminary.

Pérez, Alvaro and Maricarmen Laureano. 2000. *Formación y organización de una biblioteca teológica: Un manual para la capacitación*. San José, Costa Rica: Red Latinoamericana de Información Teológica. This is a second edition of: Pérez, Álvaro. 1992. *Manual para bibliotecas teológicas*—Theological Library Manual. San José, Costa Rica: Asociación Latinoamericana de Instituciones de Educación Teológica.

––– and Fredy Rivoir. 2000. *Directorio latinoamericano de bibliotecas y bibliotecario(a)s teológicos*. San José, Costa Rica: Red Latinoamericana de Información Teológica.

Prien, Hans-Jürgen. 1985. *La historia del cristianismo en América Latina*. Salamanca: Sígueme.

Rivera Dorado, Miguel. 2006. *El pensamiento religioso de los antiguos mayas*. Madrid: Trotta.

Zaldivar, Raul. 2006. *Teología sistemática: Desde una perspectiva latinoamericana*. Barcelona: Clie.

# CHAPTER 8

# Theological Libraries in North America

STEPHEN SWEENEY

## Introduction

"Theological libraries, in nascent form, emerged with the establishment of theological seminaries" (Hotchkiss, Graham, and Rowe 1996). Indeed, a historical sketch of theological libraries in North America can be traced as far back as the early eighteenth century. The Reverend Doctor Thomas Bray and his work in the seventeenth and eighteenth centuries is arguably the beginning in the United States of advocacy for theological libraries.

Theological schools during these two centuries, however, focused more on confessional/denominational training and did not have established standards around the education of the student until the early twentieth century. The Association of Theological Schools evolved out of a need for standard development in theological education. The later development of the American Theological Library Association helped strengthen the standards around library and information resources in theological schools and seminaries.

In his attempt to summarize the findings of a special 1960 *Library Trends* issue on "Current Trends in Theological Libraries," Decherd Turner (then of Bridwell Library at Southern Methodist University) wrote a still-timely observation of theological libraries:

> *Theological libraries are indelibly tied to theological education. Analysis and judgment in every paper in this issue springs from the ever-present question: 'What is the content, structure, and purpose of theological*

*education?' So sensitive to this foundation have been the contributors that no portion of the picture could be developed without some expression concerning the nature of theological education (Turner 1960, 281).*

The point made in this comment reflects on the critical role that theological libraries and librarians play in forming future ministers. In context, the quote by Turner was published a mere twenty-four years after the first institution of accrediting standards in theological education. Timothy Lincoln (2004) argues that "theological libraries matter because patrons need skilled specialists to assist them in minding pertinent information." He posits this argument in the context of libraries, perhaps even for North American theological libraries in particular. Some information is freely available, some are mediated by skilled professionals in libraries, and the theological librarian helps to mediate this information to students.

This short chapter will follow historical developments of theological libraries and librarianship in North America through to the creation of the Association of Theological Schools and the rise of the American Theological Library Association (today, Atla). Consideration will be given to the development of standards for the library in the theological education enterprise. Attention must also be paid to the growth of related theological librarianship organizations, some of which include the Catholic Library Association (CLA), the Association of Jewish Libraries (AJL), and the Association of Christian Librarians (ACL). Professional development and continuing education are important products of these and other library associations and will be considered as well. The final segment will provide an overview of librarianship education in North America.

## Historical Developments in Theological Education and Librarianship

Theological libraries and librarianship in North America have grown from the beginnings of colonization to the way they are lived, used, and understood today. This section attempts to, not exhaustively, trace some of that history from approximately the mid-seventeenth century through the current day. First, a look at the Reverend Doctor Thomas Bray and his contribution to the growth of public and theological libraries in England and the United States. This discussion is followed by more recent developments in theological librarianship; the Autumn 1960 issue of *Theological Education* was dedicated to this topic, as has been the topic of three twentieth-century books on theological librarianship (De Klerk and Hilgert 1980; Hotchkiss, Graham, and Rowe 1996; McMahon and Stewart 2006).

Image 1: Library of the United Lutheran Seminary, Gettysburg + Philadelphia, PA, USA.
© James Trent, United Lutheran Seminary

The Reverend Doctor Thomas Bray is recognized as an apostle for libraries in England and the United States. He helped to formally establish the Church of England in the colony of Maryland and can be identified for his contribution to the establishment of lending, parochial, and public libraries in England and the United States. He makes the case in his unpublished tract *Bibliothecae Americanae Quadripartitae*, perhaps unwittingly, for theological education and theological libraries when he says, in part, "Now the Persons whose Chief Business it is to be men of Knowledge are the Clergy, because they are to instruct others; And it is impossible they should be Able to Communicate to others, what they are not themselves first become Masters of" (quoted in Steiner 1896). The Rev. Dr. Bray is making the case for sound theological education, which requires the theological library, in order that the clergy might promote the use of libraries to the publics they serve. He contends, "I heartily wish the great Use and frequent Borrowing of Books out of these Libraries."

While Bray was already concerned with theological libraries in 1701, as late as 1969 C. Douglas Jay makes the case that theological education and theological libraries are among the slowest to adapt to changes in the environment: "And in theological schools where we are confronted with both planned and unplanned changes that few could have anticipated ten years ago, libraries and librarians are often charged with being the most reluctant to yield vested interests" (Jay 1969). This sentiment still reflects the reality for some librarians and some institutions, but many more theological libraries have embraced the pace of change and the importance of advocacy in their institutions. Some years later, Dr. Calvin Schmitt made the acerbic remark, "What do you think a librarian is? A warehouse?" (De Klerk and Hilgert 1980) One needs only consider the current North American discourse on scholarly communications in libraries, the role of librarians in the publishing process, and the specialization and contribution of theological librarians to the profession to realize the magnitude of impact being made by this community.

Calvin Schmitt was the General Director of the Jesuit-Krauss-McCormick Library in Chicago from 1975–1980, and he argued that a theological library is "simultaneously an educational expression and a servant of such an encompassing perspective" (De Klerk and Hilgert 1980). This explanation of a theological library touches many aspects of the work of librarians today. The definition extends to the library as a physical space, with all of the services provided to the various communities; it also helps collection development policies, allowing libraries to grow in denominational currency and relevance, and it reaches to human resources issues and all the attendant issues that accompany that part of library oversight. Dr. Schmitt's definition of libraries still extends to theological libraries and librarianship in North America today.

Theological libraries and librarianship have grown considerably from the time of Dr. Bray and his support and patronage of the public, lending, and parochial libraries to what continues to be seen as the critical importance of the role of libraries in theological education. Given the amount of influence libraries and librarianship have, Diener (1969) makes the astute observation: "A library can be an asset in theological education if the librarian has a clear vision of the supporting role he plays in research and the formation of the theologian. A library can be a liability if it serves only its own purposes and if its sole active role is as a purchaser in the book trade."

As the understanding of theological and academic libraries as assets to their institutions continues to develop, Atla strives to become the hub of worldwide scholarly communication in theology and religion to support this mission. One of the ways topics continue to be explored is via the Atla Annual conference. David Lewis, the Dean Emeritus of the IUPUI University Library, spoke at the closing plenary session of the 2018 Atla Annual in Indianapolis. Situated in the context of change, Lewis proposed a challenge to academic librarians, of whom this author suggests theological librarians live as a subset. While the challenge was specific to the creation of an open scholarly commons in the area of theology and religion, two of his steps resonate with the development and growth of theological libraries in North America. Point two of his four-step challenge was to make a plan. Plans are effective as living documents, engaging all appropriate stakeholders along the path. His third point was to "create the incentives and the organizational capacity to solve the collective action problem" (Lewis 2019). Theological librarians and the libraries they serve live in the context of larger institutions, recalling Schmitt's reflection on what a library is; libraries and their librarians are able to solve problems by considering their role in the space they occupy.

## *Development and Growth of Standards in Theological Education and Libraries*

"President George Horr of Newton Theological Seminary invited the leaders of other Baptist seminaries to confer on the wartime crisis, and President Abbott Lowell of Harvard then invited the assembled Baptists to form the nucleus of a larger group to meet in Cambridge in 1918" (Miller 2008). It was in 1918 that seminaries formed an association–the Conference of Theological Seminaries and Colleges of the United States and Canada, reorganized in 1936 as the American Association of Theological Schools (AATS), later to become the Association of Theological Schools (ATS) (Ziegler 1984). What this original meeting prompted continues to be found today at professional conferences, ATS biennial meetings, and cross-institution collaboration: similarities between struggles, successes, dilemmas, and the like. At their meeting in Cambridge, these seminary presidents determined the best course forward was to conduct a study on the efficacy of theological education. Securing funding from the Institute for Social and Religious Research (ISRR), they were able to proceed. The outcome was what the presidents had expected, "that something had to be done to improve seminary standards" (Miller 2008). The result of the study funded by ISRR was for the AATS to become an accrediting agency. Early on, as demonstrated further in this section, the library in the accreditation lifecycle of theological education became important.

Having been built at the end of World War I, growing through the Depression and World War II, ATS has been successful in its role as an accreditor in primary measure due to the commitment of its membership. In lesser part, but no less important, ATS has grown by the generosity of funders. From its earliest days and funding from ISRR, John D. Rockefeller, and Sealantic to a more sustainable path viewed through the lens of today, ATS has brought much to the enterprise of theological education. Important to point out, of course, is the interconnectedness of the three individuals and organizations previously named.

Image 2: Barbour Library at Pittsburgh Theological Seminary, USA. © Craig Thompson Photography & LGA Partners, LP

Theological education experienced a renewal of sorts in the post-World War II era in the United States and Canada. Libraries in this ecosystem became one of the first focal points. Between 1934–1957, several reports and studies were published with a particular level of attention paid to the library (Hotchkiss, Graham, and Rowe 1996). Shortly after the 1934 report, ATS delegates voted for the AATS to become an accrediting agency and, one biennial meeting later (1936), the first accrediting standards were published. The entire set of standards was two pages and focused on student outcomes as well as factors in the life of the institutions, including faculty resources, library resources, and financial resources. Compared to the nineteen standards in 2018 covering 98 printed pages of material, the 1936 accrediting standards were briefer. The next minor revision of the standards happened in 1954, and the library standard grew from one sentence to three pages. Tanner (2018) writes, "Only twice in the 80-some-year history of the ATS Commission have the Standards undergone a major revision or redevelopment." These two events were voted by delegates at the 1972 and 1996 biennial meetings. At its 2018 biennial meeting in Denver, ATS membership voted unanimously "to authorize the ATS Board of Commissioners to undertake a comprehensive redevelopment of the Standards of Accreditation and the Commission Policies and Procedures expeditiously and with a substantial

*Introduction to Theological Libraries*

participation process" (ATS n.d.). The proposed redevelopment of the standards is expected to be presented and voted on at the 2020 biennial meeting.

In the midst of all this development in theological education, AATS authorized the first national conference of seminary librarians at their biennial meeting in 1946. At this same meeting, delegates chose seminary libraries as the area of focus for the biennium 1946–1948. Two results were produced as a result of this work of the AATS. First, the American Theological Library Association–now known as Atla–was established and, second, the first conference of librarians was held in 1947 at Louisville Presbyterian Seminary (Hotchkiss, Graham, and Rowe 1996). More attention will be paid to Atla in the section of this chapter dedicated to that purpose.

Working in collaboration, the ATS and Atla obtained a Lilly Foundation grant to study the role and needs of libraries and librarians in theological schools in North America. The project was funded in 1981, and the primary outcome of the project was the publication in 1984 of *Theological Libraries for the Twenty-First Century: Project 2000 Final Report.* Stephen Peterson of Yale Divinity School Library was recruited to author this report. In the editorial preface of the supplement dedicated to this topic, Associate Editor for Theological Education Leon Pacala writes, "This is an important document... This document will have served its purpose if it reminds us of our responsibilities to future generations in all matters of library resources and leads us to thoughtful and deliberate responses" (Peterson 1984). Project 2000 was given a fourfold charge, and it was intended to focus on ATS member institutions as well as to inform the 1983 standards reconsideration. The fourfold charge was as follows:

1. to analyze the roles of theological libraries for the remaining decades of this century,
2. to identify the nature of the resources needed to fulfill these roles,
3. to propose strategies and programs which will assist schools in shaping library resources, and
4. to propose guidelines for development and evaluation (Peterson 1984).

Peterson wrote two follow-ups to his Project 2000 report: one in 1987 (*Project 2000 Revisited*) and one in 1990 entitled *The More Things Change—The More Things Change: Theological Libraries in the 1990s.* The conversation about libraries in the context of theological education and in the life of the ATS has continued. A 2004 issue of *Theological Education* was again dedicated to libraries and librarianship, as well as other articles and books on the topics of library standards, library resources, and theological librarianship.

## Birth and Growth of Atla and Professional Theological Librarianship Organizations

The previous section's treatment of the birth and growth of what would become the ATS pointed out a need for collaboration among seminary librarians. Early meetings of librarians discovered what still occurs at Atla and other library professional association conferences today–namely, that issues facing libraries and librarians in one institution are very relatable and translatable to issues at others. The creation of the various professional theological librarianship organizations in North America aimed to address these and other needs. In the case of Atla, a need was particularly the role of the library and information resources in accreditation.

While Atla was originally created out of an accrediting need in theological librarianship as well as a dearth of information around periodical indexing, the association has grown greatly in stature since that time. Robert Beach (1971) was asked to deliver a reminiscent speech of Atla's history at the 25th annual conference. That talk was called *Once Over Lightly* and, in it, he claims that "ATLA has not just happened! There has been a cause, a need, an exploration, an open-ended task."

In order to understand the development of Atla, it is important to see the steps that took place leading up to its creation.

Interest in the work of theological libraries and librarians has roots in the late 19th century. Ernest Cushing, in 1884, was the American Library Association's (ALA) reporter representing theological libraries. That grew, over time, to become the ALA Round Table for Theological Libraries in 1916, which later became the Round Table of Libraries of Religion and Theology. After 1924, the growing organization was renamed the Religious Books Round Table. This group continued to grow when, in the aftermath of the Second World War, AATS renewed its consideration of the library in the theological education ecosystem. The biennial meeting of the AATS in 1946 had, as one of its primary outcomes, the resolution to study theological libraries. From their meeting at McCormick Presbyterian Seminary in June of that year, they encouraged a call for a meeting of seminary librarians, and this event came to pass at Louisville Presbyterian Seminary in June 1947 (Beach 1971). More than fifty librarians were present for that first meeting in Kentucky of what would become Atla; 2019 saw almost two hundred attendees at the 72nd annual conference in Vancouver.

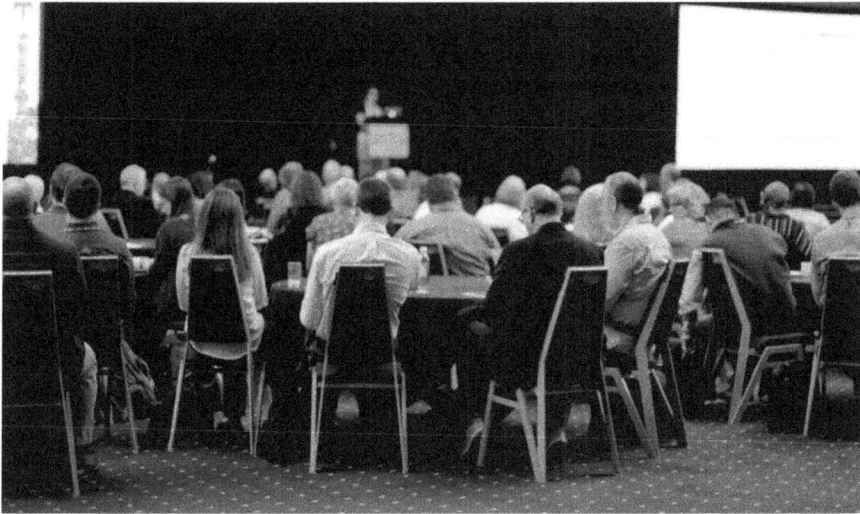

*Image 3: Plenary session at Atla Annual 2019 in Vancouver, Canada. © Atla*

Three interwoven strands came together to help Atla become the association it is today. The first was in the creation of Atla in order to strengthen the accrediting standards around library and information resources, increasing awareness of the lack of indexing in religious periodical literature, and finally came the work of recruiting qualified theological librarians to staff and fund quality theological libraries.

The American Theological Library Association was created by an act of the AATS in order to strengthen the standard around library and information resources. The 1938 AATS standard on the library in theological education was numbered as Standard 5 and read:

> *An accredited Theological Seminary or College should have a library which is live, adequate, well distributed and professionally administered, with collections bearing especially upon the subjects taught and with a definite annual appropriation for the purchase of new books and the appropriate contemporary periodicals (quoted in Tanner 2018).*

Comparatively, the forty-four words defining the Library standard are certainly terser than the nearly thousand words that identify the Library and Information Resources standard in 2018.

Next, recognizing a lack of indexing in religious periodical literature led to the creation of the ATLA Committee on Microphotography in 1949. In 1956, a grant from Sealantic Fund, Inc. of $110,000 was split into two parts; $80,000 for microtext and $30,000 for indexing (Hotchkiss, Graham, and Rowe 1996). The result of this grant, and indeed one of its requirements, was the creation of two Boards in 1957 to govern the work of the association; these were the Board of Microtext and the Board on Religious Periodical Index.

The third strand of awareness in the development of Atla into the association it is today revolved around the recruitment of qualified theological librarians for quality theological libraries. A number of developments can be traced in this vein. In 1961, an $875,000 matching grant was received from Sealantic Fund, Inc. for print resources in libraries. In 1964, $436,750 was added to this matching grant (Beach 1971). By 1968, the Lilly Foundation had funded improvement of the qualifications of theological librarians by a total of $108,000 (Hotchkiss, Graham, and Rowe 1996). 1970 saw the addition of Catholic seminary libraries joining Atla for the first time. Discussions about collaborating with Atla products and the Catholic Periodical Literature Index (CPLI) began. Atla's Library Consultation Program began in 1971 and continues to the present day. In 1979, the Boards of Microtext and Periodical Indexing came together by a vote of the respective Boards, and with that came much discussion, oversight, and involvement by the membership. As identified in the section on the ATS, the final report of Project 2000 was published in 1984 by Dr. Stephen Peterson of Yale Divinity School. In 1985, Albert Hurd was appointed Executive Director of Indexing. The growth of indexing and member services precipitated Board action such that, at the winter meeting of the Board in 1988, a Task Force for Strategic Planning was created. The charge of this task force was to engage in the process of looking at the structure for the association and to develop a strategic planning process. This work turned out three key weaknesses present in the Association:

1. the program boards and the Board of Directors functioned by combining policy formation and management roles,
2. the standing committees were hampered by their inability to enlist active membership support or to effectively address the emerging interests of theological librarianship, and
3. the lack of a CEO hampered the organization's work (Hotchkiss, Graham, and Rowe 1996).

The Board presented this information to the membership and, on Friday, June 21 at the 1991 conference in Toronto, the bylaw amendments necessary to cause these changes were passed. Albert Hurd was named CEO of Atla effective July 1991 and the governance structure of Atla changed in such a way that the Board entrusted to the CEO the daily operations of the association. This was a major milestone, as previously the Board was responsible for making daily and operational types of decisions on behalf of the Association.

There are many other notable achievements of the Association. Starting with the first conference and continuing to the present day, the Association has created and published the *Summary of Proceedings*. The *Atla Newsletter* began in 1953 and is still published online. The Atla Serials Exchange began in 1964 and is still operational. Atla has continuously worked with the AATS and its successor, the ATS, on standards around library and information resources in theological education.

Atla was originally a brainchild of the AATS in response to poor staffing, inadequate collection development policies, and the evolution of accrediting standards. This short section on the history of Atla has been intended to serve as a historical sketch of the evolution from 1938 Library standards to the robust hub of scholarly communication in theology and religion that Atla has become. Atla continues to serve its mission of fostering the study of theology and religion by enhancing the development of theological and religious studies libraries and librarianship.

Atla continues to serve the theological library and librarian community through various channels. There are three current Atla Open Press publication products: Books@Atla Open Press, *Theology Cataloging Bulletin,* and *Theological Librarianship.* Books@Atla Open Press is an expanding project that aims to publish open access books under a Creative Commons Attribution-NonCommercial license in three categories: scholarly editions, association editions, and reprints. *Theology Cataloging Bulletin* is a quarterly publication that contains information about new and changed Library of Congress Subject Headings (LCSH) and Library of Congress Classification (LCC) numbers, among other spotlights of this journal. Begun in 2008, *Theological Librarianship* is an open access journal publishing essays, columns, critical reviews, bibliographic essays, and peer-reviewed articles on various aspects of theological librarianship and its contribution to theological education.

From the Board of Microtext and the Board on Religious Periodical Index in the 1940s, Atla continues to serve its membership and customers through indexing, abstracting, and full-text resources. This takes shape through the research tools that Atla offers today. Some of those tools are the Atla Religion Database® (Atla RDB®), AtlaSerials® (Atlas®), and AtlaSerials PLUS® (Atlas PLUS®).

Alongside the beginnings of membership associations around religious and theological books and libraries, from the ALA to the AATS and the beginnings of Atla, there are other movements that were born and grew up during this same timeframe. Some of these other professional associations include the Catholic Library Association, the Association of Jewish Libraries, and the Association of Christian Librarians.

The Catholic Library Association (CLA) was established in 1921 and, according to its website:

> ...is an international membership organization, providing its members professional development through educational and networking experiences, publications, scholarships, and other services. The Catholic Library Association coordinates the exchange of ideas, provides a source of inspirational support and guidance in ethical issues related to librarianship, and offers fellowship for those who seek, serve, preserve, and share the word in all its forms.

Today, the CLA produces a variety of benefits for its members. It provides ongoing professional development and continuing education through bi-annual conferences and other means, it publishes *Catholic Library World,* and it offers a variety of awards in Catholic librarianship and theological education.

The Association of Jewish Libraries represents a merger, in 1966, of the Jewish Librarians Association and the Jewish Libraries Association. The Jewish Librarians Association was formed in 1946 to serve academic, archival, and research institutions; the Jewish Libraries Association was formed in 1962 to reach a broader base including synagogues, community centers, and smaller Jewish library and media centers. The AJL's mission is to be "an international professional organization that fosters access to information and research in all forms of media relating to all things Jewish. The Association promotes Jewish literacy and scholarship and provides a community for peer support and professional development" (AJL, n.d.). In addition to offering an annual conference for the purpose of professional development and continuing education, the AJL also claims a handful of publications, some of which include *Judaica Librarianship, AJL News & AJL Reviews,* conference proceedings, as well as a host of digital monographs.

In 1956, five librarians met to form what would ultimately become known as the Association of Christian Librarians (ACL). Their mission is "to strengthen libraries through professional development of evangelical librarians, scholarship, and spiritual encouragement for service in higher education" (ACL n.d.). The ACL meets annually at a conference in early June in locations that move around North America to reflect the breadth and depth of the evangelical Christian tradition to provide this professional development and continuing education offerings. The ACL also works to produce a variety of materials for libraries and librarians. These include the *Christian Periodical Index* (CPI), *The Christian Librarian* (TCL), the *Librarian's Manual,* and the *ABHE Library Guidelines* (Association for Biblical Higher Education).

The birth and growth of Atla, the Catholic Library Association (CLA), the Association of Jewish Libraries (AJL), and the Association of Christian Librarians (ACL) further advances the professionalization of theological librarianship in North America. These associations grew out of needs discerned by librarians in particular areas of theological education and follow in line with some of the other developments that have been considered in this chapter. All of these associations afford their membership leadership possibilities. These opportunities span the spectrum from serving on the board of an association to volunteering to lead an interest group. Along with the groups mentioned above, there are other membership opportunities for theological librarians in North America. Fifteen regional groups across the continent work closely with Atla; some receive programming and technical support from the Association to accomplish their goals of continuing education, networking, and professional development.

Because some issues of professional development and continuing education span beyond the scope solely of theological librarianship, there are other opportunities for librarians in North America as well. Local, state/province, regional, as well as national and international library associations exist to provide these opportunities. One additional opportunity for aspiring librarians as well as for professionals in the field bears mention. The iSchool at the University of Illinois offers a graduate-level course titled "Theological Librarianship" (IS 568) on a regular basis.

## Librarianship Education in North America

The growth and development of theological education and libraries in North America has been documented in other parts of this chapter. Requirements for theological librarians vary widely by the institution; some require doctoral degrees, some require theological degrees, and some require only graduate-level studies in librarianship. Librarianship education in North America, and the work of the American Library Association as an important part of that, are well chronicled.

Much like the accreditation process that grew out of the first meetings in 1918 that developed into the Association of Theological Schools, library education is accredited. "Accreditation serves to ensure educational quality, judged in terms of demonstrated results in supporting the educational development of students. Judgments are made by carefully vetted, unbiased practitioners and faculty professionals at the expert level" (ALA n.d., "Standards"). This quote from the introductory paragraphs of the *Standards for Accreditation of Master's Programs in Library and Information Studies* captures the essence of an accrediting agency.

Outside of the accreditation process, various ALA entities have knowledge and competency statements for professionals.

While recognized by the Council for Higher Education Accreditation, the ALA Office for Accreditation "serves the general public, students, employers, and library and information studies Master's programs through the promotion and advancement of education in library and information studies" (ALA n.d., "Office for Accreditation"). The most recent accrediting standards for library and information studies were passed by the ALA Council in January 2019. While the Committee on Accreditation (COA) is closely tied into the ALA structure, the COA is structured in such a way that it enables a reasonable degree of practical autonomy from their work being unduly influenced by the ALA.

The COA is comprised of twelve members by appointment, and the Chair is chosen annually from within the committee membership. Care is taken to ensure representation from among the schools accredited, recognizing that the "ALA's accreditation of LIS programs in the United States, Canada, and Puerto Rico, is voluntary, non-governmental, and collegial" (Abdullahi 2009).

As of 2017, there existed 66 ALA-accredited programs, and 61 institutions with ALA-accredited programs among 33 US states (including Washington DC and Puerto Rico). Expanding their reach across North America, five Canadian provinces were offering ALA-accredited programs. As online education continues to expand, there are 39 ALA-accredited programs offering fully online programs; these are self-reporting schools. Integral to the process of accreditation, institutions and programs must apply for status as accredited. In 2017, there were two programs with candidacy and two programs with pre-candidacy status. Across all accredited programs, 16,081 total students were enrolled in ALA-accredited programs as of the Fall term of 2017. In considering the field and potential applicants for librarian positions, ALA reports 5,863 graduates of ALA-accredited programs during the 2016–2017 academic year (ALA 2019).

The summary comment from Owens and Leonhardt (in Abdullahi 2009) captures the state of formal library education and training:

> *LIS education in North America is a growing, self-examining, and corrective process while at the same time applying sensitivity to standards and accreditation with collegiality, respect and support for the profession, an entity critical to the continuing development of LIS in North America.*

# Summary

Theological libraries have a history in North America dating back to the beginning of the eighteenth century, and theological librarians have had an important role to play in them since that time. This short chapter has attempted to trace a historical arc across North American developments in theological education that led to a particular interest in accrediting standards, the birth and growth of Atla, as well as other professional library and librarianship organizations, and a broad look at librarianship education in North America. In her introduction to the section on theological librarianship in *A Continuing Conversation* (McMahon and Stewart 2006), Anne Womack captures the work of theological librarians in North America when she says that:

> *Theological librarians are at once all these things: academic professionals with sophisticated language skills, information technology experts, building managers, budget jugglers, pastoral counselors, and stewards of our institutions' learning resources.*

# Works Cited

Abdullahi, Ismail, ed. 2009. *Global Library and Information Science: A Textbook for Students and Educators*. Munich: IFLA Publications.

American Library Association. 2019. *Prism: The Office for Accreditation Newsletter* 27, no. 1 (Spring).

———. n.d. "Office for Accreditation." Accessed February 28, 2019, *http://www.ala .org/aboutala/offices/accreditation*.

———. n.d. "Standards of Accreditation of Master's Programs in Library and Information Science." Accessed February 28, 2019, *http://www.ala.org /aboutala/offices/accreditation*.

Association of Christian Librarians. n.d. "About Us." Accessed February 28, 2019, *http://www.acl.org/index.cfm/about-acl/*.

Association of Jewish Libraries. n.d. "Mission and Goals." Accessed February 28, 2019, *https://jewishlibraries.org/Digital_Publications*.

Association of Theological Schools. n.d. "Redevelopment of ATS Commission Standards and Procedures." Accessed 28 February, 2019. *https://www.ats.edu /accrediting/overview-accrediting/redevelopment-ats-commission-standards -and-procedures*.

Beach, Robert. 1971. "Once Over Lightly: Reminiscences of ATLA from its Founding to the Present." *Atla Summary of Proceedings*: 141–151.

De Klerk, Peter and Earle Hilgert, eds. 1980. *Essays on Theological Librarianship: Presented to Calvin Henry Schmitt*. Philadelphia: American Theological Library Association.

Diener, Ronald E. 1969. "Pooling of Resources and Bibliographical Control." *Theological Education* 6, no. 1: 52–58.

Hotchkiss, Valerie, M. Patrick Graham, and Kenneth Rowe, eds. 1996. *The American Theological Library Association: Essays in Celebration of the First Fifty Years*. Evanston, IL: American Theological Library Association.

Jay, C. Douglas. "Change, Relevance, and Theological Librarianship." *Theological Librarianship* 6, no. 1 (1969): 7–14.

Lewis, David W. 2019. "Reimagining the Academic Library." *Atla Summary of Proceedings*: 19–35.

Lincoln, Timothy D. 2004. "What's a Seminary Library for?" *Theological Education* 40, no. 1: 1–10.

McMahon, Melody Layton and David R. Stewart, eds. 2006. *A Broadening Conversation: Classic Readings in Theological Librarianship*. Lanham, MD: Scarecrow.

Miller, Glenn T. 2008. *A Community of Conversation: A Retrospective of the Association of Theological Schools and Ninety Years of North American Theological Education*. Pittsburgh, PA: Association of Theological Schools.

Peterson, Stephen. 1984. "Theological Libraries for the Twenty-First Century: Project 2000 Final Report." *Theological Education* 20, no. 3, supplement.

Steiner, Bernard C. 1896. "Rev. Thomas Bray and his American Libraries." *The American Historical Review* 2, no. 1: 59–75.

Tanner, Tom. 2018. "Accreditation Standards: A Look Back and A Look Around." *Theological Education* 52, no. 1: 33–50.

Turner, Decherd, Jr. 1960. "Summary." *Library Trends* 9, no. 2 (October): 281–3.

Ziegler, Jesse H. 1984. *ATS through Two Decades: Reflections on Theological Education, 1960–1980*. Vandalia, OH: J. H. Ziegler.

CHAPTER 9

# Christian Theological Libraries in North Asia

SEOYOUNG KIM

## Introduction

This chapter will give information on the development and status of predominantly Christian theological librarianship in North Asia, concentrating on South Korea and Japan. Christianity entered Japan in 1549, 235 years before entering Korea. Although the timing and method of faith transfers were different, the Korean and Japanese churches still have many things in common, just as Korean and Japanese societies resemble each other. In the past, there was on-going persecution of Christians by the government; foreign missionaries and the spread of Christianity were seen as an invasion of a foreign power or a threat to political and social stability. In the 20ᵗʰ century, there was a constant and painful compromise between the forces of imperialism and those of nationalism. Korea, like Japan, has been very influenced by Confucianism and Buddhism; both are deeply associated with cultural traditions (Chŏng 2018).

Nevertheless, both Korea and Japan have maintained a system of Christian theological education; the seminary library has developed through foreign encouragement that began in the late 19ᵗʰ century (Cho 2011). While the Korean church has achieved rapid growth since the 1970s, the number of practicing Christians in Japan continues fairly constant at approximately 1.9 million (Iwai 2019). This chapter will cover Korea's Christian theological libraries, the Korean Theological University and Seminary Library Association (KTLA), and general library science education in South Korea in the first part, while the latter part will describe the situation in Japan, relating to theological education and libraries and librarianship education.

## South Korea

### Christian Theological Libraries in South Korea

In the 1800s and early 1900s, missionaries came to Korea from Europe, Australia, the United States, and Canada and began home-school teaching. Such study groups were the predecessors of the schools for formal theological education. In 1901, Pyongyang Presbyterian Theological Seminary (조선예수교장로회신학교) was founded by PCUSA missionary Samuel A. Moffett. Later, the foundation of theological libraries began with the establishment of seminary colleges for each denomination (Kim 2003, 12).

The number of Christians increased in the 1970s and 1980s. According to "Results of the 2015 Population and Housing Census (Population, Household, and Housing)," the religious environment of South Korea is that the population without religious affiliation increased from 47.1% in 2005 to 56.1% in 2015. The population with religious affiliation decreased from 52.9% in 2005 to 43.9% in 2015. A religious population of 43.9% means that 21,553,674 Korean people have a religious affiliation (Statistics Korea 2015, 4). Protestants in South Korea make up 19.7% of Korea's population and 45% of religious affiliation (9,675,761). Thus, Protestants have become the most numerous religion in Korea. The second most populous religion is Buddhism–15.5% of Korea's population, 35.3% of religious affiliation (7,619,332). The third one is Catholic–7.9% of Korea's population, 18% of religious affiliation (3,890,311). Thus, Christians in South Korea (Protestants and Catholics) are 27.7% of Korea's population, 63% of religious affiliation (13,566,072) (Korean Statistical Information Service, 2020).

In South Korea, as the number of Christians increased in the 1970s and 1980s, the number of theological schools and theological libraries also grew significantly. Most of the theological libraries were small and grouped together to make a theological library association. Through the association, theological librarians have been working together to actively respond to the rapid increase of information and the various information needs of users. In the following section, the Korean Theological University and Seminary Library Association will be described in detail.

In 2002, there were 38 member schools of the Korea Association of Accredited Theological Schools (전국신학대학협의회–KAATS) and, in 2003, there were 23 non-member theological schools. Thus, it was estimated that the number of seminaries was roughly 61 at that time and the number of theological libraries

*Image 1: 1907 First graduates of Pyongyang Theological Seminary.*
*(Andong Presbyterian Church 2015)*

was approximately the same (Kim 2003, 23–25).[1] According to a study of 38
theological libraries in 2015, 73.7% of libraries (28) had less than 2,000 users,
approximately one to three library staff, less than 200,000 volumes in their
collection, and less than ₩150,000,000 (US $127,242) budget for purchasing
materials. More than half of seminary libraries (73.7%) were rather small. Such
libraries have an insufficient number of librarians; these staff members have
varied responsibilities regardless of their degree, ability, or experience.

According to Yang Sŏng-gŭn's (2018, 82–83) study, there were, on average, 4.7
librarians who worked at Catholic university libraries; on average, 3.18 librarians
at small Protestant seminary libraries; and, on average, 7.75 librarians at large
Protestant seminary libraries. The major duties were acquisition and cataloging
in all libraries studied. In the libraries at Catholic universities and small
Protestant seminaries, the same person in charge of the acquisition department
also handled the general administrative affairs. Although cataloging was the

librarian's major focus, Catholic university libraries provided document delivery services actively as well. However, small Protestant seminary libraries utilized minimal human resources. Therefore, there was a real limitation to provide expertise in the subject area. On the other hand, at large Protestant seminary libraries, the cataloguing specialist undertook the cataloging task; other librarians were able to provide user-centered library services, reference services, and document delivery services, utilizing subject expertise.[2]

In the same thesis, among 52 survey responses, Yang found that 50% (26) of the librarians had only a Bachelor of Science degree in library and information science, and 23% (12) of the librarians didn't have any librarian's certificate. Only 5.8% (3) of the librarians had both library and information science and theology degrees; 78.8% (41) of the librarians didn't have experience in theological education.

As a result, the more experienced the librarian was, the more likely they were to demonstrate expertise in their field of study. Their degrees and experiences strongly influenced their understanding of the subject matter. Generally, librarians who held two degrees–library science and theology–were best equipped to provide library services requiring theological knowledge. Contrary to such an expectation, there was no difference between the education that librarians received and their duties within the library structure. Even respondents who did not have the librarian's certificate or the subject expertise performed the duties requiring that knowledge. In addition, the performance of librarians who had experience was not different from that of inexperienced librarians (Yang 2018, 80).

Despite this surprising information, Yang (2018, 81) also noticed that librarians recognized clearly the need for studying specific areas in order to work professionally in the following duties: reference service, educational support service, research support service, and acquisition. Clearly, librarians responded that in order to have a high level of performance, there was a need for specialized and advanced training.

Certainly, the important question posed is why a person without a librarian's license was allowed to work in the university library. In communication with the author, the director of the Korean Theological Library Association (KTLA) office, Kim Su-yŏn, indicated that there was a decision by the school administration to permit personnel without a librarian's certificate to perform all library duties. Later, some of those staff personnel would acquire a license through the librarians' education center. Sometimes, the staff member who studied theology came to work in the theological library and acquired the librarian's certificate through the librarian's training or degree. Kim Su-yŏn stated to the author that the duties of university librarians were not much different from personnel without the library science degree.

Furthermore, the director of the Korean Association of Private University Libraries (KAPUL), Lim Dong-gyu, acknowledged in communication with the author that as of now, none of the university library directors in Korea have a librar background. In the National University Libraries, all employees, including librarians, are civil servants. These librarians cannot be a director of a national university library; only a full professor or an associate professor is able to serve as a director. In South Korea, the library director position has been regarded as one of the university positions afforded to a tenured faculty member without experience in any or all facets of librarianship. On the other hand, in a private university, a librarian can be the library director; fifteen years ago, few university libraries had a library director who had an academic library background. However, in the last ten years, the highest level an accredited librarian can attain is the position of deputy director. Lim Dong-gyu pointed out that, because of a decrease in the student-age population, the government is reducing the number of universities and the number of college admissions. As a result, the university budget has been reduced, forcing each university library to reduce its budget as well as the staff. The director of a research institute under the Korea University and College Library Association (KUCLA), Oh Se-hoon, indicated in a telephone interview with the author that the reduced budget directly and seriously affected library staffing. Today, the proportion of yearly contracted workers, in university libraries, accounts for forty to fifty percent.

Nevertheless, recently, there is a noted change in regard to the importance of having certified librarians administering theological libraries. It is now recognized that a library directorship is an important position and should be offered to a person with advanced studies in the field of library science.

## Korean Theological University and Seminary Library Association (KTUSLA) [3]

By looking at the history and development of the Korean Theological Library Association (KTLA), now the Korean Theological and Seminary Library Association (KTUSLA), this section shows how theological librarianship has been organized and explained and how theological libraries have been cooperating in South Korea. The KTLA was launched on April 16, 1973; the association had thirteen member schools. As of 2019, the KTUSLA has a 46-year history and 52 member schools have registered. Before this association was founded, theological librarians were working only for their individual schools. However, they realized the need for intercollegiate cooperation and standardized work processes. In June of 1972, librarian Dr. Leo T. Crismon, of the Southern Baptist Theological

Image 2: Academic Information Center of SungKyul University.
Photo courtesy of Kim Su-yŏn.

Seminary Library, visited South Korea. Librarians from seminary libraries across the country were assembled. They had a meeting and agreed that a library union movement was necessary for the successful development of all library operations. After five subsequent meetings, the articles of association were drafted. The name of the association was designated as the Korean Theological Library Association and established in April 1973. After this association was founded, a seminar was held regularly. In addition, the KTLA was responsible for various kinds of publications and, as a result, the perception of the seminary library improved substantially.

Six seminars held in the 1970s focused on encouraging working-level librarians to attain basic qualifications as well as a true sense of mission as librarians. In the 1980s and the 1990s, a seminar was held twice a year. In the early 1980s, seminars were geared to enhance the professionalism of librarians. In the 1990s, most of the themes of the seminars referred to the inception of 'Library Computerization.' For example, there was an emphasis on implementing co-operation in the use of multimedia through the internet. In the 2000s, the seminars were held with a focus on sharing materials and the need to create digital information. The current director of the KTLA indicated to the author that,

*Introduction to Theological Libraries*

in the 2010s, the seminars discussed measures to prepare for evaluation according to the requirements of the university evaluation process and the implementation of the university library promotion law in 2016. In addition, there was further discussion of the role of the library in the "fourth industrial revolution."

*Theological Literature Information* (신학문헌정보) was the first publication of the KTLA. The magazine published quarterly and included news or papers from theological libraries from 1979 to 1990. In 1982, the association also published *DDC Classification Table (Religion Field: 200): Korean Translation and Original Text Table*. This book was 200 (Religion) Class Dewey Decimal Classification, 18th edition, with the translation revision in Korean. From 1984 to 1990, the union catalogue for Korean dissertations related to theology was presented. This contained bibliographic records of theological dissertations at both the master's and doctoral level submitted to universities in South Korea. The union catalogue of overseas dissertations held by each theological library was also published in 1996. Shortly after that, the age of computer electronics had arrived. After 1996, most of the printed books published by the KTLA were discontinued and switched to an electronic publication (Database). The association made CD-ROMs of dissertations of theological degrees at that time. The KTLA started a system of collaborative purchases and utilization of overseas master's and doctoral dissertations. The union catalogue of domestic and international periodicals owned by each member library was made into a database by the KTLA that could be accessed online. In addition, the KTLA produced theological e-books. According to Kim (2003, 2), there were three main categories of cooperative activities centered on the KTLA at that time: sharing acquisition, building a comprehensive bibliography database, and interlibrary loan.

In 2004, the KTLA's commemorative paper called "Theology and Library: Korean Theological Library Association 30 Years of History (신학과 도서관: 한국신학 도서관협의회 30년사 | )" was published. As of 2004, all information was accessible online, thus having no further need for print publication. In addition, the CD-ROM production of dissertations was also suspended because the Department of Education informed each candidate to upload his or her own paper to the collection. The full-text of dissertations from all over the country can be accessed online. In 2004, The KTLA joined Atla as a member. In 2015, the KTLA formed its first overseas volunteer group and began volunteering in the seminary library and the Christian school libraries of developing countries.

According to a presentation document of the 97th KTLA Winter Academic Seminar in 2015, there was a need felt to develop a project that conforms to the KTLA's mission and purpose. The idea prevailing within the overseas volunteer group was that the KTLA chose one of several libraries abroad that asked for help and sent a volunteer to the library. The volunteer would help to educate the person in charge of the library. The group also built the library WEB/DB server, the network, the web-based library operation system, and open-source software on behalf of the local staff. Volunteers helped classify books, input their metadata in the system database, and arrange the books on the shelf. While experiencing a variety of cultures, volunteers were able to broaden their own understandings of vastly different societies. For the first time, in 2015, the KTLA overseas group went to the Myanmar Reformed Presbyterian School of Theology in Myanmar in order to volunteer. Then, the group left for Indonesia to volunteer in 2018 and volunteered in Cambodia in 2019.

On January 19, 2017, the 44th regular general meeting decided to modify the name of the association from the Korean Theological Library Association to the Korean Theological University and Seminary Library Association. There were two reasons. First, when the KTLA was established in 1973, it considered only church libraries as members. However, in 2017, 100 percent of members were both theological universities as well as seminary libraries. Second, the KTLA wanted to join and receive member status in the Association of University Libraries.

The development of the KTLA resembled the stages of human development. In the beginning, the KTLA focused on the formation of the personal identity of each theological librarian. In the next phase, it published various tools, such as comprehensive catalogues, to encourage the cooperation of librarians in acquisition, cataloguing, as well as interlibrary loan. With the development of computers and the internet, the publishing project has ceased. In 2015, the KTLA launched an overseas volunteer group and helped libraries to resolve different issues of acquisition and management. Thus, we are seeing the growth and maturation of the Association as one that shares its members' experiences and skills. This degree of dedication will bring a new level of expertise to the Korean theological libraries.

Today, there are new challenges for the association. The director of the KTUSLA office pointed out in communication with the author that it was related to a decrease in the school-age population of Korea. This is what I mentioned previously; other association directors also noted this decrease to be the most influential factor in the current difficult situation of Korean university libraries. As a result, the university library budget has been reduced. This situation has also affected the Association, which has led to less involvement and participation in seminars and activities by its members. Thus, the KTLA is trying to encourage the development of both seminars as well as cooperative purchasing beneficial to all member libraries.

*Image 3: 2019 KTLA Summer Academic Seminar Participants. Photo courtesy of Kim Su-yŏn.*

## Librarianship Education in South Korea

The first educational program for librarians in Korea was offered by the National Library School at Chosun (meaning "Korea") National Library in 1946. It was a one-year course to train librarians. In 1955, Ewha Women's University started to offer courses in library science as an undergraduate minor for junior and senior students (Ŏm 1989). In 1957, the Library Science program was established at Yonsei University by library experts dispatched from George Peabody College for Teachers (Cho 2003). Some 60 years later, there are more than 30 universities that provide a library science program in South Korea (Cho 2011, 230). In detail, the librarianship education of South Korea consists of a one-year program at the School of Library Services Institute attached to Sungkyunkwan University, a two-year course at technical and junior colleges, a four-year course at colleges and universities, and master's programs and PhD programs at graduate schools. However, there are no theological librarianship programs in any university (Ŏm 1989, 220–1). According to "A Study on the Prospect of Manpower Demand and the Institutionalization of the Subject Librarian" (Sangmyung University 2008, 282–283) the current librarian education system of South Korea remains at the level of undergraduate. This is the major obstacle to activating a subject librarian such as a theological librarian in South Korea, with a lack of manpower, difficulty in the placement of personnel and staffing, and budget constraints. Currently, because of the large supply of graduates in library science, compared to the demand for librarians, graduates are forced to obtain a year-by-year contract or a temporary library placement. Thus, it is fortunate that the KTUSLA presents the seminars for librarians two times yearly. These seminars continue to give librarians opportunities for education.

## Japan

### Theological Education and Libraries in Japan

The 2015 annual statistical research on Japanese religion (Iwai 2017) shows 1.9 million Christians (1.5%), which is very small compared to 88.7 million Buddhists (69.8%) and 89.5 million Shintoists (70.4%). Japanese Buddhism is an integral part of the cultural tradition. Shintoism has preserved its guiding beliefs throughout the ages (Pak 2002, 14).

Christianity was introduced in Japan when Francis Xavier, a Jesuit priest from Spain, arrived in Kagoshima in 1549. Initially, there was interest in Western culture and the Catholic evangelical teaching of Jesuit priests. Eventually, "Toyotomi Hideyoshi, the General Samurai Politician, was aware of the foreign power at the Vatican and ordered all foreign missionaries to leave Japan in 1587. By 1650, severe persecution continued for a generation" (*Encyclopedia Britannica Online* 2019). Much later, after 1859, with the opening of the Nagasaki port, a Protestant missionary, Channing Moore Williams, was appointed the first Episcopal missionary to Japan (*Episcopal Dictionary* n.d.). Furthermore, foreign Christian missionaries of various sects engaged in social and educational projects in Japan and contributed to the introduction of European and American culture. Kobe College, one of the oldest universities in Japan, was founded by two women missionaries, Eliza Talcott and Julia Elizabeth Dudley, in 1873.

In Japan, there are relatively few universities that specialize in theology; few have independent libraries for theology. In the following, there will be a description of Japan's representative seminaries and their libraries. Doshisha University School of Theology, Sophia University, and Tokyo Union Theological Seminary are well-known as organizations of Christian theological education. Tokyo Christian University and Japan Lutheran College are also major Japanese universities that have a theology major. However, the oldest universities in Japan –Komazawa University and Ryukoku University–were established as uniquely Buddhist seminaries, and thus no Christian theological library is encountered at these two universities.

Doshisha University was established in 1875. According to its website, "Joe H. Neesima, the 'Samurai Christian,' after completing nine years of studies in the United States, returned to Japan as a missionary of the Congregational Church (currently the United Church of Christ) and established Doshisha." The Doshisha University School of Theology had originally provided only for the study of Protestant Christianity, however, in 2003, the School actively launched research into Judaism and Islam. Doshisha University has two main libraries; the Imadegawa Library and the Ranend Memorial Library. According to 2018 Statistics (Doshisha University Library 2018), they have approximately 1,046,000 books, fifteen full-time library staff members, eight contract staff, and 820,008 users per year. Currently and surprisingly, the Library Director of Doshisha University Libraries is not a professional librarian, rather a professor of economics. The Assistant Director of the Library is a professor of science and engineering. The theological library of Doshisha University is a library that belongs to the School of Theology and Graduate School of Theology. This is an independent theological library, however, three librarians in this library do not have librarian qualifications. Furthermore, according to the rules of the university, the Theology Library Director can be the dean of any university department; again, that position doesn't require library experience or education. The current Theology Library Director is a professor of philosophy and religious studies. A year's budget for books is 25,758,000 ¥ (approximately US $238,687). The theological collection volume is 120,637–11 percent of the total collection number of Doshisha University Libraries.

Sophia University is a private Jesuit research university in Tokyo. In 1908, it was founded by three Jesuit priests as the first Catholic university on the Kioi site where Sophia still stands. This school offers Catholic theology programs at undergraduate and graduate levels. According to 2018 statistics (Sophia University Library 2018), it has five libraries; Central Library, Law School Library, Shakujii Branch, Junior College Division, and Mejiro Seibo Campus Library. They have a total of 1,205,531 books. Among them, Shakujii Branch Library (27,943 books) has been the theological library but, in March 2020, Shakujii Branch Library will be closed. That's because Shakujii Branch Library's building is old and most theological classes are taking place on Yotsuya campus. Thus, currently, the theological collection was transferred to the Central Library. The Central Library will collect and house theological books. This library has a staff of fourteen; seven staff members are certified librarians. 874,127 users per year visited this library. The annual book budget (including the budget for electronic materials) is 460,000,000 ¥ (approximately US $4,262,613) and the budget for theological books is 9,000,000 ¥ (approximately US $83,398). According to the budget report, theological books account for two percent of the total book budget

Image 4: The first library of Doshisha University (1914). Photo courtesy of Jirokazu Koeda.

of the Central Library. Otherwise, as one of the research organizations, there is Kirishitan Bunko Library. This was founded in 1939 "with a mission to advance the study of the history of Kirishitan (early Japanese Christians) and the study of cultural exchanges between Japan and Europe." This library has more than 15,600 books in various languages.

Tokyo Union Theological Seminary (TUTS) includes the theological schools of the Lutherans, Baptists, and Episcopalians, and were united into one theological school during World War II. The library's collection size is 121,000 volumes; main subjects are theology, religion, and philosophy. TUTS Library has the majority of all Japanese Christian books from the Meiji period. Thus, it has the best collection of theological books in Japan. Besides, this library uses its "Tokyo Union Theological Seminary Decimal Classification Table" for classifying books.

Tokyo Christian University (TCU) is the premier Evangelical University in Japan. This school offers a Bachelor of Arts, master's, and doctoral degrees in theology for students. In 1990, TCU emerged out of a merger of three Christian schools; Shisei Jiden Women's School (偕成伝道女学校), Tokyo Christian Theological Seminary (東京基督神学校), and Tokyo Christian Junior College (東京基督教短期大学). TCU Library is also a combination of three libraries; Public Christian Research Library (共立基督教研究所図書館), Tokyo Christian Theological Seminary Library (東京基督神学校図書館), and Tokyo Christian Junior College Library (東京基督教短期大学図書館). TCU Library has approximately 80,000 books. According to the philosophy of its foundation, the library collects and houses mainly Christian and other religious materials. A year's budget is approximately 5,000,000 ¥ (US $46,332) for purchasing books and approximately 1,500,000 ¥ (US $13,899) for subscribing to journals. There is one full-time librarian; in addition, there is a part-time staff. Dr. Nobue Kuchi [木内伸嘉] has been the Library Director since April 2012.

The Japan Lutheran Theological Seminary was founded in 1909 for the purpose of training evangelists and pastors in the Lutheran faith. It became Japan Lutheran College (ルーテル学院大学) in 1996. According to its website, the two main focal points of the library collection are theology and social welfare science.

Komazawa University's history began in 1592. In Japan, there are two main Zen Buddhist traditions, Soto and Rinzai. Komazawa was a center of learning for the young monks of the Soto sect. According to its website, Komazawa University is currently trying to "cultivate students who try to introspect, learn new trends in academic studies and practice them in modern society by applying Buddhist Teachings to today's education." Komazawa University Library has 41,317,000¥ (US $382,388) budget for purchasing books (Komazawa University Library 2018, 7). The collection size is 1,020,862 volumes, except for 15,322 books of Law School (Komazawa University Library 2018, 11-12). In addition, Komazawa University has a Museum of Zen Culture and History.

Ryukoku University was founded on the principles of Jodo Shinshu Buddhism in 1639. According to the library's website, "in approximately 1655, the library not only gathered materials but also provided lending services. Entering into the 1890s, a campaign was initiated with the aim of becoming the world's largest public Buddhist library," and after the construction of an independent library in 1908, the collection of materials grew and Omiya Library was completed in 1936. At the present time, the Ryukoku University library system is comprised of three libraries: the Omiya Library with a collection focused on the humanities, the New Fukakusa Library with a collection focused on intercultural studies and sociology, and the Seta Library with a collection focused on social welfare and natural sciences. Thus, the theological collection is located in Omiya Library. Ryukoku University Omiya Library has 749,076 books and 71,893 books are checked out each year (as of March 2019).

## Librarianship Education in Japan

Japan is the country where American-style library science education was introduced at the earliest time in Asia (Cho 2011, 230). The Japan Library Association (JLA) was founded in 1892. In 1903, the JLA started the first formal training for library personnel in Japan–a program of two-week instruction. In 1917, the lectures in librarianship were first provided at a university (Ŏm 1989,

217). Before World War II, Japan's library science education policy was established by the enactment of library and librarian qualifications and the establishment of government-level librarian education institutions. However, there were limits that only the qualification of lower-level librarians was strictly defined by a qualification test; a librarian education institution was not a formal educational institution at that time (Ŏm 1989, 231). The first department of library science was established at a university in 1951, six years ahead of Korea. Keio University, the oldest private university in Japan, opened the School of Library Science, which was called Japan Library School. The School was greatly helped in its foundation by the participation of the American Library Association (Ŏm 1989, 217–18).

Currently, only five universities have been providing first-degree level library education: Keio, Tokyo, Kyoto, and Toyo Universities, and the University of Library and Information Science. This program requires 38 credits in a variety of courses. Except for these five schools, the rest of the universities offering library science courses require 19 credits (Ŏm 1989, 218–19). At present, after students acquire more than 32 credits of library science and graduate from college, they can qualify as a librarian in Japan. They don't need a double major or an advanced degree in library science, like in the United States.

Realistically, in Japan, there is very little chance to be hired as a librarian by the university. While working in the library, some employees study library science. Librarianship education is not compulsory education for working in university libraries. The library director has an analogous position to a university executive. It is quite usual that a college professor of any discipline serves as the library director. He/she is an expert in his/her research field rather than a library specialist. The term of the library director is usually two to three years. It is rare that a librarian actually becomes the library director in Japan. It is important to note that Japan has no theological library association, as well as no theological librarianship program.

## Conclusion

The theological libraries and librarians of South Korea and Japan were reviewed in this chapter. More than half of seminary libraries in South Korea are rather small. The number of employees working for such a small library is also small. Thus, regardless of the individual educational background: certificate, bachelor's, or advanced degree, every library employee has the same generalized responsibility. Japan also has little recognition of how it is important that the library is operated by a certified librarian. The result is often inadequately trained

Image 5: Central Library of Sophia. Photo courtesy of Satoko Goto.

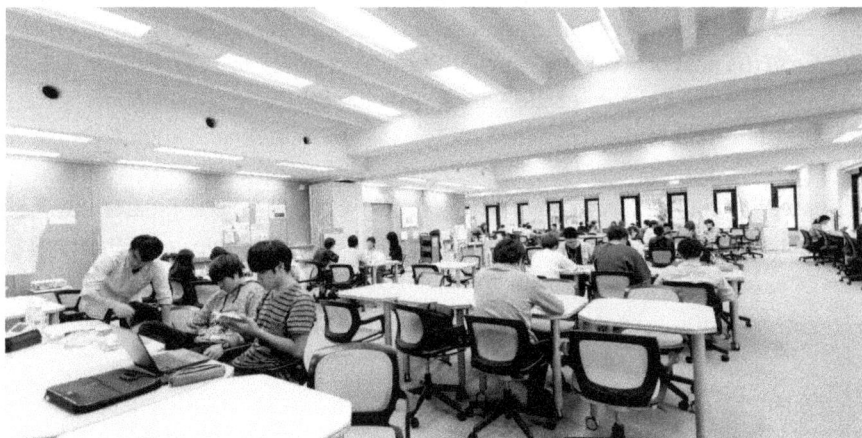

Image 6: Central Library of Sophia. Photo courtesy of Satoko Goto.

library personnel. These staff members, many without the requisite educational background, are responsible for a variety of library-related functions. The library directorship is in a very similar situation to library personnel. It is quite common that a university professor of any discipline is named head or director of a theological library in either South Korea or Japan, again without taking into consideration educational preparation for such an important position.

South Korea, unlike Japan, has a long history of supporting a theological library association. Fortunately, there is a small path towards improvement, this is found through the Korean Theological University and Seminary Library Association. This association does give serious consideration not only in regard to the materials of the collection housed in the library but also the qualifications of personnel responsible for maintaining a high quality of standards in the library for the academic community.

## Notes

1. In 2019, member schools of KAATS were 40 according to its website, but the total number of non-member schools is not recorded.
2. This study analyzed data of 28 theological school libraries of the Korean Association of Private University Libraries (한국사립대학교도서관협의회–KAPUL). The jobs of 149 librarians that belong to 28 theological libraries were analyzed. Furthermore, a survey of 52 librarians was conducted to determine their subject expertise; this thesis analyzed whether there was a relationship between the librarian's theological expertise and the librarian's duties in the library. In other words, this study attempted to discern whether a librarian with expertise in the field of theology is engaged in subject-specialized services as well.
3. In 2004, a brief history of the Korean Theological Library Association (KTLA) was published in the "도서관분야 NGO들 [Non-Profit Organizations related to Library]" section of 도서관 문화 | [*The Library Culture*] journal. This section is based on English translations of that article and KTLA's commemorative paper titled "신학과 도서관: 한국신학도서관협의회 30년사 [Theology and Library: Korean Theological Library Association 30 Years of History]."

## Works Cited

Andong Presbyterian Church. 2015. "역사 자료 [Historical Data]." *http://www .andong-ch.org/since1909photo/54487*.

Cho, Chae-sun. 2011. "일본의 학부과정 도서관학 교육 형성과정에 관한 연구 [A Study on the Developmental Process of University-based Librarianship Education in Japan]." 한국문헌정보학회지 [*Han'guk munhŏn chŏngpo hakhoeji* | *Journal of the Korean Society for Library and Information Science*] 45, no. 2: 230. *http://www .doi.org/10.4275/KSLIS.2011.45.2.229*.

Cho, Chae-sun. 2003. "우리나라 납본제도의 시작 [The Beginning of the Korean Legal Deposit]," *The Newsletter of Libraries* (March). *http://www.nl.go.kr/pds /research_data/text/newsletter/200303/200303history.htm*.

Chŏng, Da-bin. 2018. "아시아 복음화, 미래교회의 희망: 일본교회의 삼중대화 노력 1. 다종교 사회 속 일본 가톨릭; [The Evangelization toward Asia, the Hope of a Future Church: the Triple Dialogue Efforts by the Church of Japan 1. Japanese Catholicism in the Multi-religious Society]." *Catholic Times* (December 9): 11.

Doshisha University Library. 2018. 2018年度版 図書館データ集: 対象, 2018年4月 ～2019年3月 [*2018 Library Data: April 2018–March 2019*]. *https://library .doshisha.ac.jp/attach/page/LIBRARY-PAGE-JA–114/123842/file/2018.pdf*.

*Encyclopaedia Britannica Online*. 2019. S.v. "Kirishitan." *https://www.britannica .com/topic/Kirishitan#ref278402*.

*Episcopal Dictionary of the Church*. n.d. S.v. "Williams, Channing Moore." Accessed July 10, 2019, *https://www.episcopalchurch.org/library/glossary /williams-channing-moore*.

Iwai, Noriko. 2017. *Measuring Religion in Japan: ISM, NHK and JGSS*. Pew Research Center, October 11. *https://www.pewresearch.org/wp-content /uploads/sites/7/2017/11/Religion20171117.pdf*.

Kim, Hyŏn-ju. 2003. "우리나라 신학대학도서관의 협력활동에 관한 연구 [A Study on Cooperative Activities among Libraries of Korean Theological Universities]." Master's thesis, Chungang University.

Komazawa University Library. 2018. 駒澤大学図書館, 平成30年度図書館年次報告 書 [*Komazawa University Library, 2018 Library Annual Report*]. *https://www .komazawa-u.ac.jp/facilities/library/files/nenpou_h30_1.pdf*.

Korean Statistical Information Service. 2015. 성별,연령별, 종교별 인구 (시군구) [2015 Population Census by Gender, Age, Religion (Si, Gun, Gu)], 인구총조사 [Population Census] *http://kosis.kr/statHtml/statHtml.do?orgId=101&tblId=DT _1PM1502&conn_path=I2*.

Ŏm, Yŏng-e. 1989. "Library Education in Japan, the Republic of Korea and Taiwan: A Comparative Study (I)." *Tosŏgwanhak* 17 (December): 219–220.

Pak, Chŏng-su. 2002. "성약시대 일본선교의 토착화 전략에 관한 연구 [A Study on the Strategy for the Settlement in Japan of Missions of the Completed Testament Age]. Master's thesis, Graduate School of Theology, Sun Moon University.

Sangmyung University. 2008. 최종보고서: 주제전문사서 인력수급 전망 및 제도화 방안 연구 [*Final Paper: A Study on the Prospect of Manpower Demand and the Institutionalization of the Subject Librarian*]. The National Library of Korea. *http://policy.nl.go.kr/cmmn/FileDown.do?atchFileId = 212977&fileSn = 54492*.

Statistics Korea. 2015. "Results of the 2015 Population and Housing Census (population, household and housing)." *http://kostat.go.kr/portal/eng /pressReleases/1/index.board?bmode = download&bSeq = &aSeq = 361147&ord = 1*.

Sophia University Library. 2018.図書館蔵書冊数、雑誌・新聞タイトル数 / *Library* [*The Number of Titles in Library Collections: Books, Journals, and Newspapers*]. *https://www.sophia.ac.jp/eng/aboutsophia/overview /u9gsah0000000am6-att/Statistics2018p16Library.pdf*.

Yang Sŏng-gŭn. 2018. "신학대학도서관 사서의 주제전문성과 직무 현황에 관한 연구 [A Study on the Subject Specialist and Job Status of Librarians of Both the Theological Seminary Libraries and the Theological University Libraries in South Korea]." Master's thesis, Incheon National University.

# CHAPTER 10

# Christian Theological Libraries in South Asia

YESAN SELLAN

## Introduction

This chapter outlines the history and development of Christian theological libraries in South Asia. Geographically, Asia occupies one-third of the land area of the earth and 60% of the world population. Although Asia gave birth to Christianity, the development of theological libraries in the South Asia region is uneven. The theological education in this region, which these theological libraries support, is broadly classified into Ecumenical, Evangelical, and Charismatic. This chapter briefly narrates the contribution of South Asian theological associations and foundations and other regional agencies and networks as they relate to the development of theological libraries and regional library associations. The chapter ends with a synopsis of the current realities facing theological libraries and librarians in Asia and suggestions for strengthening the ongoing relationships.

## Christian Theological Education and Libraries in India

Among South Asian countries, India is the largest and most populated country. Buddhist institutions of Taxila and Nalanda were the earliest learning centres of higher education, which existed in India during the first century AD. The earliest libraries in Buddhist monasteries, temples, and mosques have had their greatest contribution to the religious instruction and training of priests (Gul and Khan

2008). Bimal Kumar Datta's (1960) study elicits the historical development of libraries in the ancient and medieval periods in India. Datta noted that, from the 10th century onwards, temples became chief centres of learning. Muslim rulers and sultans had maintained libraries within the premises of temples and palaces. Taher (1994, 270–74) noted that oriental libraries had the support of kings Tipu Sultan, Raja Sarfoji, and other nobles. Tanjore Saraswati Mahal Library, the Royal Asiatic Society Library, Kudha Bakhsh Library, and the Theosophical Society library are some of the most-known examples from this period. Later libraries of temples, monasteries, and others became targets during the foreign invasion of Muslim leaders, Arabs, and sultanates, and a means of destroying Indian history, culture and religious identity.

The history of Christianity in India is traditionally associated with the Apostle Thomas. The Syrian Church of South India is one of the most ancient churches of Christendom and is by far the oldest Christian community in India (Ranson 1945, 32). Two years before the arrival of Francis Xavier to found the Jesuit Mission of India in 1542, a seminary in Cranganore, near Cochin, was founded by Franciscan fathers in 1540 to prepare persons for pastoral ministry. The establishment of this seminary was historically important for the beginning of modern theological training in India. Later, in Goa, the Seminary College of St. Paul was founded, which was then taken over by the Jesuits (Neill 1984). In 1584, a seminary was established in the area of the Thomas Christians in Malabar to educate the priesthood and prepare the way for consolidating the work of the church by establishing a regular parish organization among Thomas Christians. According to the survey by Kramarek, Guant, and Sordo-Palacios (2017), it is estimated that India, with its 295 seminaries, has the highest number of Catholic seminaries in the Asia region.

A few important Catholic seminaries in India are: 1) Jnana Deepa Vidyapeeth (JDV), formerly the Papal Seminary, located in Pune, which is more than 125 years old. The Papal Seminary was originally founded by Pope Leo XIII in Kandy in 1893 and moved to Pune in 1955. JDV library holds more than 100,000 books and 25,000 bound volumes of journals. 2) Sacred Heart Theological College library in Shillong, founded in 1928, is one of the largest Catholic libraries in Northeast India, which has over 80,000 books and journals. 3) The St. Peter's Pontifical Seminary Library, Bangalore, in South India, has more than 85,000 books, journals, and other resources. 4) The Dharamarm Vidya Kshetram Library (DVK) in Bangalore is another notable Catholic library that holds over 100,000 books and journals.

Image 1: The library of the Dharmaram Vidya Kshetram (DVK). © DVK

Historically, Protestant Indian theological education was started in an informal way. Bartholomäus Ziegenbalg, the first Lutheran missionary who arrived in Tranquebar, started a seminary to train the workers for Christian work in 1705. The arrival of the Serampore Trio (William Carey, William Ward, and Joshua Marshman) at Serampore in 1810 paved the way for the modern missionary movement and the establishment of organized theological education in India. In 1818, William Carey and his friends started Serampore College to train native Christians and offer degree programmes. Favoured with the Royal Charter issued by the King of Denmark in 1827, this school had a special place among pioneering theological institutions in India. In 1918, the Bengal government passed the Serampore College Act, enabling the Council of Serampore College to exercise its authority to confer degrees. Around this time in 1824, the East India Company founded Bishop's College in Kolkata (then Calcutta) to train candidates for the ministry of the church.

Image 2: The library of the South Asia Institute of Advanced Christian Studies (SAIACS).
© SAIACS

The beginning of the 20th century was very important in the life of Protestant theological education in India, as it saw a revival that contributed to its growth and development. The need for higher theological education was fulfilled by the founding of the United Theological College (UTC) in 1910 with the support of the London Missionary Society, the Wesleyan Methodist Missionary Society, and the Arcot Lutheran Reformed Church in America. Later on, Leonard Theological College (LTC) in Jabalpur was founded with the support of the Methodist Church in 1922. In 1937, the World Gospel Mission, a holiness faith mission from the USA, founded South India Bible Institute, an interdenominational seminary, at Bangarapet.

Protestant theological education in India today is accredited by two major bodies: the Senate of Serampore College (SSC) and the Asia Theological Association (ATA). At present, 59 theological colleges in India, Sri Lanka, Bangladesh, and Nepal are affiliated with the SSC. The ATA was founded in 1970 to function as an accreditation agency to support Evangelical biblical theology scholarship and spiritual formation in Asia. It has 282 institutions as its members from 34 nations. Theological colleges accredited by the ATA offer Master of Divinity (MDiv), Master of Theology (MTh), and Doctor of Philosophy (PhD) degree programmes. Both the ATA and the SSC, as well the Association for Theological Education in South East Asia (ATESEA), have mandated their member institutions to appoint qualified librarians in theological institutions.

The largest and most important Protestant libraries in India are located in South India. Believers Church Theological Seminary Library, located in Thiruvalla, holds over 150,000 books and represents the largest Protestant theological library in Asia. Next comes the United Theological College (UTC) Library in Bangalore, with over 100,000 volumes, and then the South Asia Institute of Advanced Christian Studies (SAIACS) library, also in Bangalore, and Gurukul Lutheran Theological College and Seminary library, located in Chennai, both with a collection of 60,000 items. In North India, the largest Protestant libraries are the libraries of the Union Biblical Seminary in Pune and the New Theological College Library in Dehradun.

## Theological Education and Libraries in Bangladesh, Nepal, and Sri Lanka

### Bangladesh

Christianity in Bangladesh is more than 500 years old, yet formal theological education was started only in the late 19th century. Bishop College, an Anglican theological institution, founded in 1820 by the Bishop of Kolkata, laid the beginning of theological education in Bangladesh (Das 2012). Das noted that sixteen theological institutions in Bangladesh are broadly categorized as Ecumenical, Evangelical, Pentecostal, and others. They are members of the Bangladesh Theological Association. Libraries in these theological institutions lack learning resources and qualified staff to manage. Due to the lack of funding, the acquisition of books in these institutions is always a challenge, and donations from overseas organizations are a major support for them. No formal interlibrary loan or resource sharing is present among these institutions. Computerized cataloging systems and the internet are yet to be implemented. Andrews Theological College is the only college affiliated to the Senate of Serampore College and the College of Christian Theology is accredited by the ATA.

### Nepal

At present, Nepal has ten theological institutions; most of them were started in the late 1970s. In order to fulfill the need for offering higher theological education in Nepal, Asia Graduate School of Theology Nepal (AGSTNP) was founded in 2017. Before 2017, India, other Asian, or Western countries were destinations for Nepalis to have a theological education. The oldest theological institution is Nepal Theological College, founded in 1978 and accredited by the ATA (Tamang 2012). Most of the other theological libraries are relatively small and do not have trained librarians. The largest theological library in Nepal is the library of the

Association Theological Education Network (ATEN). The ATEN library has over 20,000 books and journals and members from various theological institutions in Nepal. At the end of the librarians' training in May 2017, the Nepal Theological Library Association (NTLA) was formed. The NTLA plans to meet twice a year and would like to develop an effective interlibrary loan system to share resources among its members.

## Pakistan

Islam is the state religion in Pakistan and Islamic theological seminaries play an important role in social, political, and religious life in this country. It is estimated that Pakistan has 30,000 *madrasas*, or Islamic seminaries (Kamil 2012). Christian theological education in Pakistan is 134 years old. The oldest theological seminary is Gujranwala Theological Seminary (GTS), formerly named Presbyterian Theological Seminary, which started in 1877 at Sialkot and was founded by the Church Missionary Society. After it moved to Gujranwala, it was renamed in 1912 as Gujranwala Theological Seminary. Prior to GTS, St. John's Divinity College was founded in 1869 by Church Mission Society missionaries and was closed after a decade. St. Paul's College in Allahabad was started in 1882. St. Thomas Theological College (TTC) in Karachi was formed in 1987. GTS has contributed immensely to the church in Pakistan. GTS and TTC could not meet the ongoing need for theological education, and therefore new theological institutions were started. Theological institutions in Pakistan lack quality faculty members, libraries, and facilities. The absence of quality literary resources and lack of cooperation among theological institutions pose a great threat to the quality of theological education. The majority of the faculty members are non-natives and the available theological literature is produced by Westerners. Nurturing indigenous thinking and the lack of support for scholarship is a challenge.

## Sri Lanka

One of the oldest Catholic seminaries in Sri Lanka is the National Seminary of Philosophate, founded in 1890 by Pope Leo XIII. Most of the churches in Sri Lanka depended on the United Theological College (UTC) in Bangalore, India, for their theological education. Anglicans sent their candidates to Bishop's College, Kolkata, Methodists went to UTC, and Baptists to Serampore College for theological training (Illangasinghe 2012). In 1963, Methodists, Anglicans, and Baptists jointly founded the Theological College of Lanka (TCL) to equip candidates for their pastoral ministry. The Ceylon Bible Institute, which was later known as the Assemblies of God Bible College, was founded in 1930 to cater to the Pentecostal churches. The majority of theological libraries, with the exception of the major colleges, do not have an adequate budget to acquire resources for theological programmes. Sharing of resources, library staff skill development, and lack of finance are some of the problems faced by theological institutions in Sri Lanka.

## Collection Development, Automation, and ICT Infrastructure

The scarcity of learning resources and dependence on donations for collection development is a major characteristic of theological libraries in South Asia. The situation has not changed much since the 1960s, when Harrison (1957, 39) and Allen (1960, 221-60) conducted two surveys on library conditions in major seminaries in Africa, Asia, and Latin America. These surveys reported the poor quality of theological collections and the lack of enough library staff as the biggest problems for libraries in South Asia.

When it comes to automation and ICT infrastructure, theological libraries in South Asia continue to strive hard to grow at par with their counterparts in other fields of study. Computerisation of libraries was once considered a luxury and now it has become essential. Support was offered by the author to over 30 theological libraries in India and Nepal for implementing computerized library catalogue systems using the open-source software KOHA and NewGenLib. Sellan and Sornam (2013) observed that theological colleges in Bangalore made significant use of information communication tools, such as the use of social media and others for their library services. This study further offered various suggestions by the respondents for improvement, which include a need for better internet connections and development of a digital library. There is already an effort among Bangalore theological libraries to establish institutional repositories for content management (Sellan, Sornam, and Naik 2014).

The Board of Theological Education of the Senate of Serampore College (BTESSC) took the initiative to bring theological librarians from institutions affiliated to the Senate of Serampore College to offer training on digital library systems and computerization. The Indian Theological Library Association organized a one-day consultation in 2007 on classification and cataloging issues faced by librarians. This was attended by twenty theological librarians from various parts of India. The consultation facilitated librarians to maintain uniformity in assigning Dewey Decimal Classification numbers for books on contemporary issues.

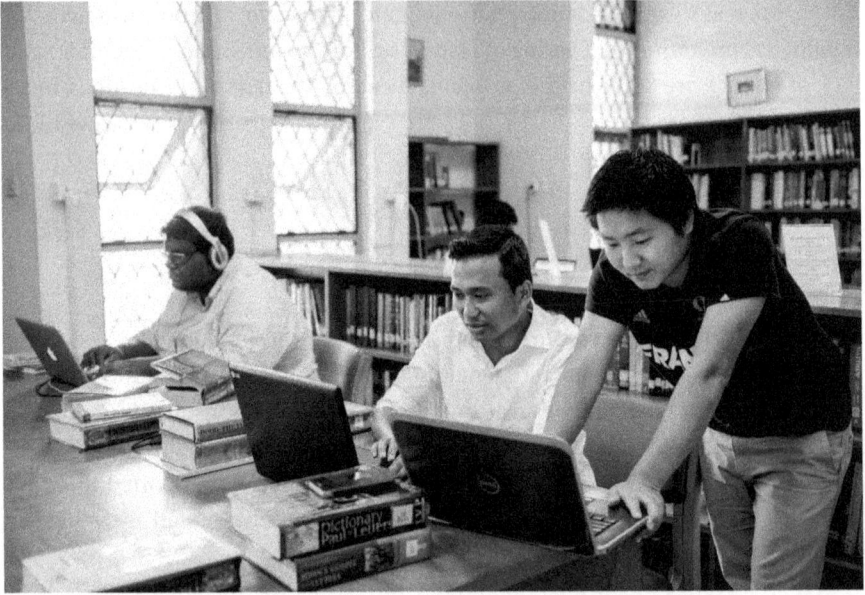

Image 3: Users in the library of the South Asia Institute of Advanced Christian Studies. (SAIACS) © SAIACS

## Staffing and Training

The contribution of theological librarians is indubitable in training men and women for the ministry of God. It is expected of theological librarians to have general library science education and also ample knowledge in theology and religious studies in order to manage theological resources efficiently and meet the information needs of theological educators and learners. The quality of theological education is closely associated with library development. The Theological Education Fund (TEF) and the Foundation for Theological Education in South East Asia (FTESEA) have been making efforts to improve the quality of theological libraries in Asia by way of supporting initiatives such as library consultations, theological librarianship courses, and recruitment of qualified librarians (Theological Education Fund 1965, 51). In response to the need for equipping theological library staff, structured theological librarianship programmes were introduced with the support of national library associations, regional networks, and various theological institutions in Asia.

In the early 1990s, the need for developing theological librarians' training was felt. In 1995 the Joint Library Committee in Bangalore had planned to offer a 6–12 week training at the South Asia Institute of Advanced Christian Studies (SAIACS) (Harris 1997). This could not be implemented due to various challenges, but it was from 1998 onwards that a formal education in theological librarianship was offered at Lutheran Theological Seminary (LTS), Hong Kong (Sui Tung 2013). At present, LTS offers a Diploma in Theological Librarianship, Master of Arts in Theological Librarianship, and MDiv and MA specialized in Theological Librarianship.

A training for theological library staff was once again resurrected at the Indian Theological Library Association (ITLA) conference held in 2002. In response to this demand, a five-week librarians' training programme was organized in 2006 at the Union Biblical Seminary, Pune. This training programme was developed by Chacko Chakco, the president of the ITLA. Experienced librarians from various Indian theological seminaries were involved in teaching, and the training was attended by sixteen participants from different theological institutions in India.

Another training programme was offered in 2010, under the leadership of the Rev. Stephenson, librarian of Southern Asia Bible College (SABC). This training was attended by 30 librarians from South India; the majority of them were from Assemblies of God theological institutions. After this training, there were no training programmes offered at SABC. Notably, the majority of theological colleges and seminaries that belong to ecumenical, evangelical, and Pentecostal categories are located in South India (Sellan and Sornam 2018).

Since 2012, the South Asia Institute of Advanced Christian Studies (SAIACS) has offered a three-month course called Certificate in Theological Librarianship (CTL). This programme has been well-received by theological colleges in South Asia to train their library staff. So far, over 60 librarians have been trained through this programme. This course is recognized by the ATA, BTESSC, and other theological accrediting associations in South Asia.

Realizing the need for training of Nepali theological librarians, Asia Graduate School of Theology Nepal, with the collaboration of the Association of Christian Librarians (ACL), organized a two-week training programme in May 2017. The training was attended by thirteen librarians from various theological institutions in Nepal.

Image 4: First generation of Certificate in Theological Librarianship graduates in 2012 at SAIACS. © Yesan Sellan

Image 5: First Nepal Theological Librarians' Training in Kathmandu, Nepal in 2017. © Yesan Sellan

*Introduction to Theological Libraries*

## Theological Library Associations and Supporting Organizations

Theological library associations and networks and other supporting agencies have also contributed to the development of theological librarianship at the Asian level.

### Forum of Asian Theological Librarians (ForATL)

Karmito (2005, 24) narrates the history of the formation of the Forum of Asian Theological Librarians (ForATL). The ForATL was founded in 1991 by Karmito (then librarian of Duta Wacana Christian University, Indonesia). Librarians from India, Indonesia, Singapore, and Taiwan gathered for a consultation in Ching Mai in May 1991, under the guidance of the Programme for Theology and Cultures in Asia (PTCA) (Pryor and Little 1993). Even today, the PTCA continues to support the cause of development of libraries. The first meeting of the ForATL was held on October 1991 in Singapore and resolved to prepare a directory of theological libraries and librarians, offer short-term training and workshops, and prepare guidelines for theological libraries in Asia. Today, the ForATL has over sixteen institutions as its members from all over Asia. The ForATL meets every three years in different parts of Southeast Asia. Publication of a thesis directory and of periodicals holdings are underway. The ATESEA and the FTESEA were major supporters of ForATL activities. The recent ForATL conferences were not represented by librarians of India, Pakistan, Sri Lanka, and Bangladesh, due to the lack of funds available for travel grants.

### Joint Library Committee (JLC), Bangalore

The JLC is one of the regional library networks in India. A consultation on co-operative library development was held on October 27, 1984, at the United Theological College, Bangalore under the leadership of Prof. F. S. Downs, the then-Convener of the UTC library committee. A joint committee of librarians of co-operating institutions was established at that meeting and decided to meet four times a year. It was decided that this committee would be known as "The Joint Library Committee, Bangalore." Fr. M. K. Kuriakose, UTC Archivist, was elected as Convener. Over the years, the JLC has had several remarkable achievements, including the publication of the *Handbook with Listing of Periodicals and Dissertations of JLC Libraries* (Patmury 1996) and others. The need to formulate guidelines for the future course of action was felt by the JLC. As a result of this, the JLC adopted its constitution and bylaws on 21 November 2002 in the meeting held at SABC. Today, the JLC has eighteen colleges as its members. It is one of the active theological librarians' forums in South Asia, which meets

Image 6: The meeting of the Joint Library Committee (JLC) in Bangalore in 2015. © Yesan Sellan

Image 7: Triennial Conference of ITLA held in Bangalore, October 4-7, 2005. © ITLA

three times a year. The JLC has launched its union catalogue online (*http://jlcbangalore.in/*), which holds over 200,000 bibliographic records from Bangalore libraries.

### Indian Theological Library Association (ITLA)

The Senate of Serampore College hosted an All India Theological Librarians conference at the United Theological College in January 1980, under the leadership of C. R. W. David. This meeting was attended by eighteen librarians from colleges affiliated to the Senate of Serampore College (David 1980, 2). The participants of this conference named this meeting as the Indian Theological Library Association (ITLA). They felt the need for inclusion of librarians from other streams of theological institutions in India, such as Catholic seminaries, Evangelical institutions, and others, as its members. It was decided to meet every three years but, due to various challenges, the ITLA could not meet regularly as decided. After a long gap, the ITLA hosted its 2nd triennial conference in Pune, at Union Biblical Seminary in October 2002. Gordon Harris (2004) describes his experience in attending the second conference of the ITLA under the theme, The *Role of Librarian in the 21st Century*. This conference was attended by over 30 librarians from various theological seminaries and colleges from India. The ITLA hosted its 3rd conference in Bangalore in 2005. Since this conference, the ITLA has not hosted another conference.

## Challenges and Suggestions

The road ahead of theological libraries in Asia is not so easy, as they are faced with limited budget provisions, lack of resources to address contextual theological issues, growing costs of periodicals, and unfavourable political scenarios in various countries in which Christians are a minority community. Also, the lack of cooperation between libraries can be a stumbling block for development. In this context, the up-skilling of theological librarians and enhancement of knowledge in the latest technologies would create ample opportunities for collaborations with libraries in the global north and mutual benefit. Networking, collaboration, and resource sharing among regional, national, and local levels provide opportunities for theological libraries to reap the benefit of resource sharing. As recommended by Harrison (1957, 53), the subscription of current periodicals and interlibrary loan systems among libraries would be the greatest service to the theological community. The use of open source solutions for computerization and developing institutional repositories helps theological libraries to grow at par with libraries in other fields of study. Globethics.net, an online global theological library (Stückelberger and Vallotton 2010) opens up scope for Global South scholarship to be widely known to the global community. Full-text theses and dissertations from Asian seminaries would be of the greatest value for global scholars to access from anywhere if they are made available in open access platforms. Open access to theological scholarship from the Global South will be a great value to the study of Christianity in Asia.

## Works Cited

Allen, Yorke. 1960. *A Seminary Survey: A Listing and Review of the Activities of the Theological Schools and Major Seminaries Located in Africa, Asia, and Latin America Which Are Training Men to Serve as Ordained Ministers and Priests in the Protestant, Roman Catholic, and Eastern Churches.* New York: Harper.

Das, David Anirudha. 2012. "Bangladesh." *The Ecumenical Review* 64, no. 2: 169–76. *https://doi.org/10.1111/j.1758–6623.2012.00159.x.*

Datta, Bimal Kumar. 1960. *Libraries and Librarianship of Ancient and Medieval India. http://archive.org/details/in.ernet.dli.2015.98910.*

David, C. R. W., ed. 1980. *Study Papers of the Seminar of Librarians of Theological Colleges in India.* Serampore: Senate Serampore College.

Gul, Sumeer and Samina Khan. 2008. "Growth and Development of Oriental Libraries in India." *Library Philosophy and Practice (e-Journal). https://digitalcommons.unl.edu/libphilprac/182.*

Harris, Gordon. 2004. "The Indian Theological Library Association Conference 2002." *Bulletin of the Association of British Theological & Philosophical Libraries* (June). *https://biblicalstudies.org.uk/pdf/abtapl/11–02.pdf.*

———. 1997. "Cooperation between Bangalore Theological College Libraries, and the Potential of Electronic Networking." *Ministerial Formation* 76 (January): 49–53.

Harrison, M. H. 1957. *After Ten Years: A Report on Theological Education in India.* Nagpur: National Christian Council of India.

Illangasinghe, Kumara. 2012. "Sri Lanka." *The Ecumenical Review* 64, no. 2: 177–86. *https://doi.org/10.1111/j.1758–6623.2012.00160.x.*

Kamil, Maysood. 2012. "Pakistan." *The Ecumenical Review* 64, no. 2: 147–59. *https://doi.org/10.1111/j.1758–6623.2012.00157.x.*

Karmito. 2005. "Forum of Asian Theological Librarians (ForATL): A Brief Historical Narrative." *Bulletin of the Association of British Theological & Philosophical Libraries* 12, no. 1 (March). *https://biblicalstudies.org.uk/pdf/abtapl/12–01.pdf.*

Kramarek, Michal J., Thomas P. Gaunt, and Santiago Sordo-Palacios. 2017. *Global Directory of Catholic Seminaries.* Washington, DC: Center for Applied Research in the Apostolate, Georgetown University. *https://cara.georgetown.edu/Part%20I%20General%20Overview.pdf.*

Neill, Stephen. 1984. *A History of Christianity in India: The Beginnings to AD 1707*. London: Cambridge University Press.

Patmury, Joseph, ed. 1996. *Handbook with Listing of Periodicals and Dissertations of JLC Libraries*. Bangalore: Joint Library Committee.

Pryor, Lynn and Jeanette Little. 1993. "Libraries and Librarians in the Asia-Pacific Region." *ANZTLA EJournal* 21: 16–21. *https://doi.org/10.31046/anztla.v0i21.929*.

Ranson, Charles W. 1945. *The Christian Minister in India, His Vocation and Training: A Study Based on a Survey of Theological Education by the National Christian Council*. London and Redhill: Lutterworth Press.

––– and S. Ally Sornam. 2018. "User Education in Theological Institutions in South India." In *International Conference on Knowledge Organisation in Academic Libraries (I-KOAL 2018): Participation of Academic Libraries in Knowledge Economy*, 127–37. Hyderabad: Manakin Press.

Sellan, Yesan, S. Ally Sornam, and K. G. Jayarama Naik. 2014. "Institutional Repositories (IRs) for Content Management in Bangalore Theological Libraries: Prospects and Challenges." In *Library Space and Content Management for Networked Society*, 192–200. Dharmaram Publications, Bangalore.

––– and S. Ally Sornam. 2013. "The Impact of Information Communication Technology (ICT) on Library Services in Select Theological Libraries in Bangalore: A Study." *Journal of Contemporary Christian* 5, no. 2: 44–61.

Stückelberger, Christoph and Amélie Vallotton. 2010. "The Future Role of Online Libraries: Globethics.Net's Innovative Model." In *Handbook of Theological Education in World Christianity: Theological Perspectives, Regional Surveys, Ecumenical Trends*, 307–12. Eugene, OR: Wipf and Stock.

Sui Tung, Tang. 2013. "The Ecumenical Landscape of Asian Theological Library Networks." In *Asian Handbook for Theological Education and Ecumenism*, 669–75. Regnum Studies in Global Christianity. Eugene, OR: Wipf and Stock.

Taher, Mohamed. 1994. "India." In *Encyclopedia of Library History*, edited by Wayne A. Wiegand and Donald G. Davis, Jr. Garland Reference Library of Social Science 503. London: Routledge.

Tamang, Ganesh. 2012. "Some Critical Observations for Theological Education in Nepal: Nepal." *The Ecumenical Review* 64, no. 2 (July 2012): 132–43. *https://doi.org/10.1111/j.1758–6623.2012.00155_2.x*.

Theological Education Fund. 1965. *Issues in Theological Education, 1964–1965, Asia, Africa, Latin America: A Report of the Theological Education Fund*. New York: The Theological Education Fund.

# Contributors

**CARISSE MICKEY BERRYHILL, PH.D.,** is Special Collections Librarian at Abilene Christian University's Brown Library. Before coming to ACU, she was Associate Librarian at Harding School of Theology in Memphis, TN (1992–2004), and Professor of English at Lubbock Christian University (1975–1992). Berryhill holds advanced degrees in English, library science, and church history. She does research in rhetoric in the Stone-Campbell religious reform movement of the 19th century and its 18th-century Scottish roots. Berryhill has received ACU's Faculty Service Award (2017), Pepperdine University's Distinguished Christian Service Award for her efforts in preservation of Stone-Campbell history (2011), and has three times received the Excellence in Online Teaching Award from the WISE consortium of library schools for her Theological Librarianship course at the University of Illinois (2007, 2009, 2012). She currently serves as chair of the Corporation Board of *Restoration Quarterly.*

**KERRIE BURN** is the Library Manager at Mannix Library, Catholic Theological College, a member institution of the University of Divinity located in Melbourne, Australia. She also chairs the Library Committee for the University and manages its online Library Hub. Kerrie has worked in theological libraries for almost twenty years, as well as in library and research support roles in the Australian university sector (Southern Cross University and Australian Catholic University). She holds a Bachelor of Science Degree and a Graduate Diploma in Library and Information Studies from the University of Melbourne. In 2018 she attained the status of ALIA Distinguished Certified Professional, an achievement recognized by the Australian Library and Information Association. Kerrie completed a Master of Arts by Research in 2007 through the then Melbourne College of Divinity, and has research and publication interests in the areas of collaborative collection development, library history, and the management of library special collections.

**KELLY CAMPBELL** is Associate Dean of Information Services and Director of the Library at the John Bulow Campbell Library, Columbia Theological Seminary in Georgia. She has worked in a variety of educational and library settings, including public and private schools and large and small public libraries. Kelly serves as a member of the Association of Theological Schools Accreditation Teams and has served in numerous leadership roles for Atla (established in 1946 as the American Theological Library Association). Holding a Doctor of Education in Organizational Leadership from Pepperdine University, Kelly is passionate about equipping people for learning and providing high-quality service.

**MATINA ĆURIĆ** is the secretary and Board member of the European Theological Library Association (BETH) and a librarian at the library of the Pontifical Mission Society in Aachen, Germany. She has fifteen years of experience working in specialized academic and ecclesiastical theological libraries in her homeland, Croatia, and Germany. Matina holds a bachelor's degree in theology and a master's degree in library science.

**ANDREW KECK** is the Executive Director of Strategic Initiatives and Special Assistant to the Dean of Perkins School of Theology at Southern Methodist University in Texas. He has worked in theological libraries professionally for almost twenty years with an increasing number of responsibilities outside of the library in accreditation, assessment, and planning. Andrew has served in numerous leadership roles for Atla (established in 1946 as the American Theological Library Association), including service on the Board of Directors. His professional interests have included exploring the vocation of theological librarians, publishing (including the journal *Theological Librarianship*), digitization efforts, digital repositories, and scholarly communication.

**SEOYOUNG KIM** is an Assistant Professor of Research and Writing, Director of Institutional Research, and Librarian at the World Mission University Library, World Mission University in Los Angeles, California. She has worked in a variety of library settings, including academic as well as church libraries. She holds a Bachelor of Science Degree in Library and Information Studies from the Duksung Women's University in South Korea. She completed two Master's Degrees of Library and Information Science: the first from Chung-Ang University in South Korea and the most recent one from San Jose State University in San Jose, California. In addition, through her studies and work, she has acquired a valuable understanding of divergent cultures. She continues to provide research support that incorporates the most advanced information literacy.

**EPHRAIM MUDAVE** is the University Librarian at Africa International University in Nairobi, Kenya. He is a member of the University Management Board and a Peer Reviewer with the Commission for University Education on Library matters. He is the Patron of the Christian Association of Librarians in Africa-Kenya. Ephraim has worked in Theological libraries for more than 24 years, mostly in management positions. He completed his PhD in Information Studies in 2016 from the University of Kwazulu-Natal in South Africa. He also holds an MA in Missions Studies from Africa International University, a Master of Library Science from Indiana University, Bloomington, and a BSc in Information Sciences from Moi University, Eldoret.

**KATHARINA PENNER** was born in Soviet Kyrgyzstan and moved to Germany as a teenager. She holds two Master's degrees–in Theology as well as in Library and Information studies–and works toward a PhD degree in Theological Education. For the past 28 years, she has worked at theological schools in St. Petersburg, Russia, in Prague, Czech Republic, and in Austria, as a faculty member as well as library director. Currently, she serves as Coordinator for Library Development at the Eurasian Accrediting Association and is involved in several writing projects as an author as well as a coordinator.

**ALVARO PÉREZ** has been a librarian at Latin American Biblical University, a facilitator for various Latin American theological librarianship workshops, Co-founder of the Latin American Theological Network (librarians' association). He has also been President of the Costa Rica Library Association, MLIS Postgraduate professor at the University of Costa Rica, Director of the *Library and Information Science Journal*, and facilitator of various Latin American Theological Librarian congresses. Other experiences include being a member of the editorial board of the *Journal of Religious & Theological Information*, a member of the Atla Advisory Board of *Theological Librarianship* (Journal), and the author of books and articles (general and theological librarianship-related).

**YESAN SELLAN** is Chief Librarian at South Asia Institute of Advanced Christian Studies (SAIACS), a premier theological institution in South Asia offering postgraduate and doctoral programs in biblical, theological, and missiological studies. Prior to joining SAIACS, he was a librarian at Serampore College, a college founded by English missionaries (William Carey, Joshua Marshman, and William Ward) in 1818. Yesan holds a master's degree in Library and Information Science

(MLISc) and a PG Diploma in Library Automation and Networking (PGDLAN). He has over twenty years of experience as a theological librarian and helped to develop a theological librarianship course at SAIACS. He was Secretary to the Forum of Asian Theological Librarians (ForATL) during 2009–15 and served as Executive Secretary to the Indian Theological Library Association (ITLA). He has completed a PhD in Library and Information Science from Bharathidasan University, a state university in Tamil Nadu, India.

**STEPHEN SWEENEY** is the Director of the Library at Saint John Vianney Theological Seminary in Denver, Colorado, USA. He serves on the Board of Directors for Atla. He is adjunct faculty at the University of Denver's Library and Information Science Program, teaching Management of Information Organizations. He completed his Master of Library and Information Science at the University of Denver in 2007 and has worked for many years in theological libraries. Spanning a career of almost twenty years, he has also worked at the Regis University Libraries as well as the Denver Public Library.

www.ingramcontent.com/pod-product-compliance
Lightning Source LLC
Chambersburg PA
CBHW031433270326
41930CB00007B/680